TURN YOUR CRAFT INTO YOUR BUSINESS™

The*Savvy*Actor®
Career Manual

By Jodie Bentley and Kevin Urban

The Savvy Actor Career Manual

by Jodie Bentley and Kevin Urban

©2010 The Savvy Actor, Inc.

For information on how to obtain a copy of this publication, call 212-502-0908 or send an email to jk@thesavvyactor.com

ISBN-13:
978-0615625263 (The Savvy Actor)

ISBN-10:
0615625266

Testimonials

"*The Savvy Actor Career Manual* is a valuable tool for anyone looking to be a professional, working actor. Jodie and Kevin combine their extensive performing experience and business know-how to help actors succeed in a most competitive field. They help performers set realistic goals and marketing plans that work. I have been a casting director for 15 years would highly recommend this manual to actors looking to take their career to the next level."

> **– Jamibeth Margolis, CSA** Casting Director

"I was able to work collaboratively with Jodie and Kevin to develop a program that suited the needs of our students. **The Savvy Actor** is a way in, and helps actors approach their careers pragmatically. It promotes sound business practices that help young artists see themselves as the industry will see them - an invaluable tool."

> **– Scott Plate**, Department Chair – Music Theatre, Baldwin-Wallace College

"While talent is an absolute given, awareness and insight into the 'business' of show business is the component that is too often ignored, misunderstood, and undervalued. Jodie & Kevin fill that gap with a simple and positive approach that teaches an actor how to brand and market oneself with confidence. *The Savvy Actor Career Manual* is an essential part of an actor's preparation."

> **– Gary John La Rosa,** Director/Choreographer

"I'm a huge supporter of **The Savvy Actor** and the dead-on coaching provided by Jodie & Kevin. There are a lot of businesses, coaches, small companies, etc., that will take your money and don't have your best interests at heart. Kevin & Jodie are the real deal. They really listen and are interested in helping. I've seen actors transform with the help of their seminars. *The Savvy Actor Career Manual* is a valuable resource to any actor out there."

> **– Jillian Sanders**, Former Agent, Don Buchwald and Associates

"I have been working with Broadway professionals for almost 15 years in New York City and I have never worked with a company that better prepares an actor for the business side of acting than **The Savvy Actor**. Jodie and Kevin are passionate about getting their clients to powerful career outcomes and their career manual is a terrific foundational tool for every actor at any level."

> **– VP Boyle,** Broadway Coach & Owner, MaxTheatrix LLC

"**The Savvy Actor Career Manual** is the most timely and helpful of the "business how-to" books of any I have ever seen. I'm working through the book myself!"

> **– Caryn West**, Audition Coach and Actor

"**The Savvy Actor** revolutionized how I market myself as an actor. One of the best tools in their manual is creating a branding statement. The first time I used my branding statement in a cover letter, I got an audition and booked the job! And Jodie and Kevin are both working actors which means a lot to me because they practice what they preach."

> **– Lynda Berge**, Actor

The Savvy Actor mission is to empower actors to think like small business owners by creating and implementing an effective business plan, branding their unique product, and developing marketing strategies that get them noticed and in the door: ultimately merging career and life into one, filled with abundance and success.

As co-founders of The Savvy Actor, Inc, Jodie Bentley and Kevin Urban have over 20 years of combined experience in the acting business in New York City. Kevin has a BA in Communications with a concentration in public relations and a theater minor. Before moving to New York, Kevin worked in marketing and business development for a financial institution. Jodie graduated from NYU's Tisch School of the Arts with a BFA in Acting. Jodie also built her own successful marketing and sales company from the ground up. They bring their passion, knowledge, and hands-on business experience to **The Savvy Actor**.

Jodie and Kevin are currently adjunct professors at Pace University and on faculty at the New York Film Academy. With their company, **The Savvy Actor,** they regularly lead workshops for other universities and professional acting schools like New York University, Baldwin Wallace, UC Irvine, The York Theatre, Weist Barron, The PIT, and The Network.

Their passion is helping actors to become successful savvy business people and empowering them with the skills necessary to compete in 'the biz' today.

Acknowledgement

First of all, we must thank those who believed in us and our business from the very beginning: Brian Blythe, Valerie Adami, Jaye Maynard, Howard Emanuel, Joseph Perniciaro, Paul Michael, Christina Shipp, Doug Shapiro, Stephen Mitchell Brown, Stacey Tavor, Jocelyn Keynes, Jamibeth Margolis, Gary John La Rosa, James Morgan, Alison Franck, George Brescia, our first mastermind group – VP Boyle and DJ Salisbury, and Michael Schaefer our editor extraordinaire (and Jodie's husband!).

We must also thank all of our amazingly talented savvy clients. It is through you and for you that this manual was born. Without you, it never would have come to fruition. In recognition of this, we dedicate *The Savvy Actor Career Manual* to you.

Thank you all for your devotion, encouragement and belief in what we do. You are our inspiration.

Foreword

There's such a thrill to being an actor. No two days are alike, zipping from one audition to another, working survival jobs, meeting industry contacts, grabbing coffee with friends to catch up on business and, of course, staying sharp: taking classes, rehearsing, and performing. With that excitement comes the necessity to master the art of balance.

To give you an idea of why we created this manual, here's a story of two actors: One went to a great acting school in NYC. The other actor came to NYC to pursue his acting passion having a public relations degree. After graduating, the acting major booked work right away and felt like her career was going to be a piece of cake. The PR major left a job in marketing and business development because even though he liked it, something was missing. He got his equity card within six months. He felt like this acting career was going to be a piece of cake too.

After a year of touring and working out of town, the acting major moved back to the city and started auditioning. She found a temp job, then a hostess job, then a marketing and sales job, and eventually started her own marketing and sales company. She burned herself out going to every audition without a clear plan. She eventually stopped altogether; she was making good money with her sales company. The PR major realized all the talent he was up against and he stopped auditioning. He took as many classes as he could, getting lost in *Class-land* for several years because he felt he wasn't ready.

They approached their acting careers from different directions but they had one thing in common – they were trying to do it all, without a plan, and went into *overwhelm.* That's where many actors find themselves – feeling overwhelmed or lost. They're spinning their wheels, leaving success to chance with no clear plan other than 'being an actor.'

Beyond craft, actors need both business skills and a plan, to guide their career. Like acting, voice, and dance techniques, business skills are a system of rules that you can practice. Learning them, practicing them, will ultimately allow your instincts to kick in and your creativity to flow. With a business plan in place, you'll have a career that is structured, consistent, and thriving. You will be a small business owner.

It was the acting major's success as a business owner that ultimately led to her acting success. She learned that by having a plan and implementing it with consistent marketing strategies, success would come. The PR major knew studying craft is crucial; that's why he focused on acting technique. In school he had already learned business skills, time management, negotiation, and all about marketing. But it wasn't until he finally applied these skills to his acting career that his success came.

It was their life experience applied with their understanding of a systematic approach to success that took their careers to the next level. It made them working actors. And if you haven't already guessed it, ideal business partners.

When you decided to follow your acting dream, the notion of being an entrepreneur and starting a business probably never crossed your mind – it certainly didn't cross ours. We were the ones who were overwhelmed and lost. When we realized it was imperative to treat our careers as a business, to map out a plan with goals, to define our products, to embrace marketing those products, and to create strategic, effective systems – our careers took off – fast. So fast that we created **The Savvy Actor** to empower other actors to do the same.

If you ever felt like we did, and you wished there was a manual on how to run your acting business, this is it. We've taken the fundamentals of a business plan and created a system that's specific for actors. This manual will be the foundation for your ultimate success. Everything about the business of your career is consolidated in this book, your one-year business plan, *The Savvy Actor Career Manual*.

Much Success,
Jodie Bentley and Kevin Urban

> *"Artists tend to leave many things up to fate, but a small business owner won't. A small business owner has a specific reason for everything they do. They also have a systemized plan. A business plan."* **– The Savvy Actor**

At **The Savvy Actor,** we look to outside sources and companies beyond our acting world to find what works and what it takes to be successful. When we started The Savvy Actor, Inc., we realized why actors never put a business plan together. All the examples of a business plan we found were overwhelming and geared toward the financial world or investors. To fill the void, we created a plan that is accessible to actors by simplifying the fundamentals of a business plan. The following are the seven sections crucial to an actor's business plan.

1. Long Term Vision: Your Passion

This is the vision for your life and for your career. It is being able to envision 1 year, 5 years, 10 years, 20 years into the future to define your life's big picture. This includes a declaration – a statement of your desires, how you're going to achieve those desires, and just as importantly, how you're going to give back to your community.

2. Goals • Projects • Tasks: The Nitty-Gritty

For most actors, everything has to happen now. They spread themselves too thin and try to do it all – TV, Film, Theater, Musical Theater, Commercials, etc. Goals must be defined. Most people can only focus on three to five goals at a time without going into overwhelm. In your business plan, you'll focus on two career goals, one life goal, and one financial goal. You will then implement those chosen goals by creating specific projects and tasks.

3. Branding: The Foundation

Most people in the industry refer too simplistically to an actor's type. We talk about the power of a brand. It's the most crucial yet empowering piece of the puzzle that people often leave out. In order to market yourself effectively, you must know what you're selling. As an actor, your brand is really your essence. It's who you are, no matter if you're hanging with your friends, auditioning, or meeting an agent at a party. It's the constant that you always bring with you, from the initial headshot, to the follow up, to getting in the door.

A brand is also a promise. A promise that the actor who comes across someone's desk in a photo is the same as who comes through door and who can be counted on to deliver over and over again. Consistency fulfills the brand promise.

4. Marketing: The Strategy

The Savvy Actor definition of marketing is: ***The creative promotion of your essence, your relationships and your successes.*** Everything you do to promote yourself and your career is encompassed under marketing. You need specific marketing strategies for your individual career goals and brand. Marketing includes: Audition Material, Headshot, Resume, Targeted Mailings Plan, Cover Letters, Postcards, Business Cards, Thank You Cards, Press Kit, Websites, Reels, Social Networking Sites, Meetings and Interviews. Each medium has a different strategy. You are in control of your marketing and need to create your strategy.

5. Support System: The Fun Part

What we are really talking about in this section is networking. But we prefer to say, "enriching your support system." It's your team of people - Coaches, Teachers, Accountants, Doctors, Fans, Friends, Peers, etc. This is not a go-it-alone-mentality business. Actors are often afraid to reach out, but you need other people's help to achieve your goals.

6. Finances: The Backbone

You need to know where you are financially. You need money to live, whether in NYC, LA, Chicago, Toronto or anywhere else. Debt is easy to accumulate and you can't run away from it or avoid it once you have it. A financial plan is important and it starts with research. How much income do you need to live? What percentage of your income are you setting aside to fund your acting expenses, living expenses, and savings for the future? You must also come to terms with your emotions surrounding money.

7. Organizational Systems: The Necessity

To be a consistent and efficient actor you need to be organized. Having organizational systems for your contacts, mailings, mobile office, home office, calendar, email, computer files, task lists, etc., is integral to running a successful business.

Start at the beginning and follow the instructions carefully.

The manual is set up to work linearly. Start with the Long Term Vision section and work your way forward. However, if finances are a major concern, you may start there. But again, start from the beginning. Don't skip ahead within a section.

The Business Plan Checklist serves as the table of contents to your business plan and once an exercise is completed you can check it off here. This will also track your progress.

This is your manual for your acting career. This is a living, breathing document. Nothing about it is etched in stone. Your brand, priorities and goals will change. Allow for it. That does not mean that you should change for the sake of change. Every decision you make must have a reason behind it.

We suggest spending at least an hour a day working on your business. Business skills need to be practiced and setting aside an hour will help focus you on your business.

Other Supplies

- ❏ A three hole punch
- ❏ Highlighters
- ❏ Tape
- ❏ Page Protectors
- ❏ Binders
- ❏ Notebooks
- ❏ Paper Clips
- ❏ Staples
- ❏ Pencils
- ❏ Pens
- ❏ Press Kit Packaging
- ❏ Resume Paper (Cut to 8x10)
- ❏ Printer Ink
- ❏ Printer Paper
- ❏ 13-Tab Expandable Pocket Folder
- ❏ File Folders
- ❏ Label Maker

Business Plan Checklist

1. Long Term Vision — pages 12 – 23

	Date Completed
• Career Self Evaluation	
• Be/Do/Have Exercise	
• 20 Year Plan	
• Declaration	

2. Goals • Projects • Tasks — pages 24 – 49

	Date Completed
• Priority Sheet and Analysis	
• Career Goal 1	
• Projects and Tasks	
• Career Goal 2	
• Projects and Tasks	
• Life Goal	
• Projects and Tasks	
• Financial Goal	
• Projects and Tasks	
• Year Map	
• Incorporate Your Calendar	
• Categorized Task List	
• Career Plan Overview	

3. Branding — pages 50 – 57

	Date Completed
• Basic Type	
• Personal Brand Breakdown	
• Brand Tally Sheet	
• Branding Statement	
• Image That Reflects your Brand	
• Wardrobe	
• Hair	
• Makeup	

		Date Completed
4. Marketing	pages 58 – 94	
Marketing Material		
• Audition Material		
• Monologues		
• Songs		
• Commercial Copy		
• Sides		
• Headshot That Reflects Brand		
• Commercial		
• Legit		
• Resume		
• Cover Letters		
• Agent		
• Submission Letter		
• Postcards		
• Thank You Cards		
• Business Cards		
Mailings Plan/Strategy	pages 71 – 77	
• Targeted List		
• Legit Agents		
• Commercial Agents		
• Casting Director		
• Theaters, Production Co's, Ad Agencies, etc.		
• Mailings Plan To Agents		
• Mailings Plan To Casting Directors		
• Mailings Plan To Theaters, Production Co's, Ad Agencies, etc.		
• Maintenance List		
• CD's, Agents, Theaters, Directors, etc.		
• Checked Out Savvy Industry Database		
Interviews	pages 78 – 90	
• Interview Questions		
• The Savvy Press Kit		
• 30 Second Blurb		
• Meeting and Interview Prep		
Online Strategy	pages 91 – 94	
• Social Networking		
• Website		
• Reel		
• Demo		

Business Plan Checklist

5. Support System	pages 95 – 103	Date Completed
• Support System Worksheet		
• Fans		
• Extended Network		
• Core Team Of Advisors		
• Enriching Your Support System		
• Maintaining Your Support System		
• Maintaining Agent Relationships		

6. Finances	pages 104 – 120	Date Completed
• Fixed Expenses Vs. Variable Expenses		
• Fixed Monthly Expenses		
• Fixed Annual Expenses		
• Total Monthly Fixed Expenses		
• Average Weekly Fixed Expenses		
• Variable Expenses Tracking		
• Financial System		
• Career Budget		
• Yearly Acting Expenses		
• Business Receipts Filing Portfolio		

7. Organizational Systems	pages 121 – 133	Date Completed
• Weekly Checklist		
• Savvy Portfolio		
• Mobile Office		
• Home Office		
• Computer Filing System		
• Email Organization		
• Audition Tracking		
• Checked Out iPerform		
• Audition Quantification		
• TV/Film		
• Commercial		
• Theater		

8. Resources	pages 134 – End	Date Completed
• The Savvy Audition Checklist		
• Vision Board		
• Success Journal		
• Affirmations		

Self Evaluation

Before you start to plan your career, you have to know where you are now, in both your life and your acting career. Be honest with yourself as you answer these questions. This is the start of your roadmap.

Your Strengths

Write down at least five personal strengths. *(both career and life)*

Your Weaknesses

Write down at least five personal weaknesses. *(both career and life)*

Your Challenges

Write down any and all challenges you have been facing. *(both career and life)*

Section 1:
Long Term Vision

Long Term Vision

You have to know what you want in order to know where you're going and how to get there. You are a complex person with a career AND a life. You're not an actor and an administrative assistant, or an actor and a waiter – but a whole human being. Your art informs your life and your life informs art.

Many actors get tunnel vision and focus solely on their careers. But it's important to know what you want in your life as well as your career. We'd like you to focus on your life as a whole. Let go of self-imposed restrictions, think big, and discover the things that you would love to be, do, and have in life.

What is it that is going to get you out of bed everyday to implement your plan? You need to connect with what drives you and what you're passionate about.

Be, Do, Have Instructions

Examine what you want to be, do, and have in your life. Write in stream of consciousness, no judging, no second-guessing. Be specific and think big!

1. **Be** - Take 10 minutes and write down everything you want to be in your life.

   For example - I want to be a mom, be respected, be written about in theater history books, be admired, be a Tony winner, be an amazing friend, be a world renowned vocalist, be a world traveler, be a Broadway star, etc.

   NOTE: Don't just write, "be happy." Happiness is a state of being, but it means something different for everyone. What would you have to be in order to be happy?

2. **Do** - Take 10 minutes and write down everything you want to do in your life.

   For example - I want to travel to Egypt, learn Italian, learn tap dancing, climb a mountain, invest in stocks, get married, see a show every week, run a marathon, take myself to the movies once a month, meet friends for coffee every week, star in an independent film, etc.

3. **Have** - Take 10 minutes and write down everything you want to have in your life.

   For example - I want to have an apartment in LA and NY, to have a BMW Z3, have a dog, have an Emmy, have a career in stage and film, have children, have a fabulous wardrobe of clothes I love, have a life partner, have an amazing support system of friends, etc.

   Note: 'Have' can mean material things of course, but make sure to include the intangible – have authenticity in all I do, have respect among my peers, have integrity, have a household name, etc.

"The blank page gives us the right to dream." – **Gaston Bachelard**, French Philosopher

---

For Example - I want to be written about in theater history books. I want to be a mom or dad.

For Example - I want to visit every baseball stadium in the US. I want to learn French.

For Example - I want to have integrity. I want an Audi TT Convertible. I want a home in Tuscany.

Be, Do, Have - Analysis

You've spent the last half hour writing. Now it's time to analyze the exercise.

Did you have any surprises?

You probably noticed some overlap in each section. That's fine. Certain ideas will come up more than once. Take it as a sign that those ideas are things that you want to manifest in your life – and maybe something you're really passionate about.

What did you find most difficult? Really think about it – which one was the hardest for you?

- Be
- Do
- Have

If you found Be the hardest: You are most likely a Do-er. You are excellent at what we call 'task lists' (to do lists) and have an amazing drive to get things done. Challenge yourself to take time to just *be*. Focus on your big picture so you don't get burnt out by the day-to-day grind.

If you found Do the hardest: You are most likely a Be-er. You are excellent at thinking big and creating ideas – putting those ideas into action may trip you up a bit. Challenge yourself when you move forward to the goals section to honor the task list and write everything down.

If you found Have the hardest: Challenge yourself through affirmations, declarations, and other releasing techniques to own the fact that you deserve to have all that you want in your life.

This exercise was about exploring your passion, and passion is something that needs to be checked in with and nurtured. We urge you to do this exercise every six months to reconnect with what you are passionate about in your life.

Now that you are thinking in terms of the big picture, it's time to get more specific. If you know precisely what you want and by when, you can determine what steps to take, and then it's just a matter of time. Success becomes inevitable.

For example, if you want to drive to LA from NY you'll need a map. In order to reach LA there are certain parts of the country you need to go through. You can go via Florida or Chicago. Either way, you'll have to cross the Mississippi River. It doesn't matter the route, you will eventually get there if you pass certain mile markers.

For this exercise consider 20 years your destination. In order to arrive at that destination, what will have had to occur? Think of 10 years, 5 years 1 years and 6 months as milestones or markers.

20 Year Plan Instructions

Write down where you want to be in 20 years, 10 years, 5 years, 1 Year, and 6 Months. Take 15 minutes and begin writing your milestones. This will be the foundation for your goal work in the next section. Be specific. For each time frame write:

Two Career Milestones

What would you like to have accomplished by this point in your career.

One Financial Milestone

By financial milestone, we mean maybe earning a particular amount, or maybe it's just opening and contributing consistently to an IRA, or saving $5000, whatever it means for you.

One Life Milestone

A life milestone could be traveling, spending more time with loved ones or taking more time for yourself. What does it mean to you?

Think back on everything you want to be, do and have, and let's map out this life – your life. Refer back to the Be, Do, and Have exercise pages. If you said that you want to own a vacation home in Cape Cod, when could that realistically happen (in your plan) given your current circumstances? Would it be now, a year from now, 10 years from now? Don't judge your ideas, just think big and incorporate your life dreams. Let this be an exercise in instinct. Go with your gut and don't over-think.

Tips On Mapping Your Milestones:

- Milestones should be in the present tense.
  Example - I star in my first Broadway show vs. I would like to star in my first Broadway show.
- Focus on what you want, not what you don't want.
  Example - I make my living solely from acting vs. I don't want to make my living waiting tables.
- Be as specific as possible.
  Example - I visit my family in Helsinki, Finland, Take an African Safari with Nicole and family, and visit Evie in the Philippines vs. I travel the world.

20 Year Milestones:

Career

Financial

Life

Your 20 Year Plan

10 Year Milestones:

Career

Financial

Life

5 Year Milestones:

Career

Financial

Life

20 Year Plan

1 Year Milestones:

Career

Financial

Life

6 Month Milestones:

Career

Financial

Life

Declaration

> *"Definiteness of purpose is the point from which one must begin. It is the knowledge of what one wants, and a burning desire to possess it. Knowing what you want is the first and, perhaps, the most important step towards the development of persistence. A strong motive forces you to surmount many difficulties."* — **Napoleon Hill,** Think & Grow Rich

Now it's time to create your declaration, or your "definiteness of purpose." It should be a statement that reflects what you want to achieve in your life and what you are going to give back to your peers, your community, and even the world. It's a powerful statement that will fuel your desire and keep you on track for your purpose in life.

Write your Declaration. Use our examples as a guideline.

Your declaration is really your mission statement for your own small business. Put this statement in a place where you will see it everyday or say it aloud every morning. Use it as a tool to focus you and to remind you why you are doing what you are doing.

Examples:

I, **Jodie Bentley**, am utterly committed to embody freedom and ease, calm and confidence, and passion and persistence in all that I do in my career and my life. I will go the extra mile in all areas with a positive mental attitude and a heart filled with love, joy, gratitude, compassion, hope, and faith, to bring abundance and success to myself and to others.

I will be a Tony™ Award-winning Broadway leading lady playing great leading lady roles in American musical theater and drama, and original roles in inspiring and brilliant new musical theater works and plays, a sitcom star that brings depth and joy into the lives of millions of people, and a familiar face commercially. I will inspire people through my art and empower thousands of actors through **The Savvy Actor** to realize they can achieve their dreams and live up to their fullest potential. I will have a yearly income from my acting, investments, residuals, and **The Savvy Actor,** of $1,000,000. I will use my wealth to help breast cancer research, the ASPCA and the Association of Retarded Citizens. I will continue to have a conscious, loving relationship with my best friend, amazing husband, and life partner, Michael.

I, **Kevin Urban**, am determined to live my life actively with a creative spirit, making healthy choices for both my mind and body, while working with others to achieve both collective and individual goals. I want to be disciplined and respected in my craft, love and be loved unconditionally, give generously of my time and money, while serving my family, my peers and my community.

More specifically, I will have a career that takes me to see the world via both stage (a Broadway musical) and screen (filmed and screened abroad). **The Savvy Actor** will have taught thousands of actors how to transform their craft into their business. I will have multiple income streams, which will include The Savvy Actor, Inc., as well as, other investments-making me a millionaire in 10 years. Using my wealth, I will donate my time and money to foundations supporting children's hospitals, cancer research, and other young entrepreneurs.

Declaration

I, _____, am

Section 2:
Goals • Projects • Tasks

Now that you have created the milestones in your 20 Year Plan, it's time to determine your specific goals. Specificity is the key to achieving any goal.

We believe people can focus on three to five goals at a time without going into overwhelm. In terms of the business plan, you're going to focus on four goals: two career, one life, one financial. You can't do everything at once; you have to pick a focus.

So let's start by determining your priorities.

> *"You have to decide what your highest priorities are and have the courage -- pleasantly, smilingly, non-apologetically -- to say 'no' to other things. And the way you do that is by having a bigger 'yes' burning inside."* – **Dr. Stephen Covey**, The 7 Habits of Highly Effective People.

Priority Sheet Instructions

Looking at the Priority Sheet, on the left side are the priorities as far as your career goals. On the right side are the craft priorities you will focus on to make those goals happen.

Thinking in terms of the next year, go with your gut, and number only 1 – 5 on each side (1 being the highest priority.) Choose five, total, per column. Take exactly one minute to complete this exercise.

Savvy Downloadable Worksheets

Register your Career Manual at **http://www.thesavvyactor.com/RegisterYourManual.php** to receive access to downloadable excel files for the worksheets contained in this section.

1. Career Goal Worksheet
2. Life Goal Worksheet
3. Financial Goal Worksheet
4. Year Map
5. Categorized Task List
6. Career Plan Overview

Priority Sheet

Number 1-5 your top 5 Career priorities and top 5 Craft Priorities, one being your highest priority. Use the extra spaces to add anything that might be missing.

No.	Career Priorities	No.	Craft Priorities
	Cabaret		Acting Business
	Comedy - Improv		Aerial Work (Trapeze, silks, etc.)
	Comedy - Sketch Writing		Audition Technique
	Comedy - Stand Up		Build Your Song Book
	Commercial - Industrials		Clowning
	Commercial - On Camera		Cold Reading Technique
	Commercial - Print		Comedy/Sitcom Technique
	Commercial - Voiceovers		Commercial Technique
	Dance		Creating Cabaret Act
	Develop Craft		Creating One Person Show
	Film - Feature Film		Dance
	Film - Independent Film		Dialects
	Film - Student/Short Films		Film/TV Technique
	Hosting		Gymnastics
	Modeling		Improv
	One Person Show		Monologues
	Recording Artist		Musical Instruments
	Theater - Broadway		Puppetry
	Theater - Build Resume – Stock & Off-Off Broadway		Shakespeare
	Theater - Off- Broadway		Sight Reading
	Theater - Readings & Workshops of New Work		Singing Voice
	Theater - Regional Theater		Sketch Writing
	Theater - Tours		Soap Technique
	TV - Daytime		Speaking Voice
	TV - Primetime		Stage Combat
	TV - Sitcoms		Voiceover Technique

Goals • Projects • Tasks

Priority Sheet Analysis

After you complete the exercise write your top five career priorities and top five craft priorities in the table below.

Career Priorities	Craft Priorities
1.	1.
2.	2.
3.	3.
4.	4.
5.	5.

Ask yourself:

- Are these career priorities what I REALLY want to focus on this year?
- Why did I list my career priorities in this order?
- Do the craft priorities correspond with the career priorities I've selected?
- Why am I focusing on these areas of craft? Why are they important to me?

Make any necessary changes so that your career priorities excite you. The areas of craft you've chosen should complement your career priorities (i.e. if film is your top career priority, then singing should not be your top skill to work on.)

Cross out the bottom two in each category – concern yourself with only the top three as you move on to defining your goals.

Goals

A goal in itself is not an active plan. When creating goals, we like to think in terms of:

- Goal: A Culmination of Projects
- Projects: A Series of Tasks
- Tasks: Actionable Steps

Completing tasks lead to the completion of a project, which in turn, leads to hitting that goal. I can't just "get an agent," but I can make a phone call to set up an appointment – one task of many to achieve a goal. (See our Career Goal Example)

To determine what your specific career goals are for the next year – look back to your Priority Sheet Analysis and your 20 Year Plan. Transfer the following to the table below.

Career Goal Analysis Table

Career Priorities:
1.
2.
3.
Six Month Career Milestones:
1.
2.
One Year Career Milestones:
1.
2.

What determines a "good" goal?

A "good" goal should:

Trigger Your Passion: You must be passionate about your goal. When a goal triggers your passion, then your level of commitment, dedication, and perseverance will be limitless. Passion will be your ultimate motivation. *For example* – Is it working with an amazing commercial agent or booking a national commercial? A commercial agent can lead to the national commercial and a national commercial can lead to an amazing commercial agent – but what is it that motivates you?

Be Definable and Visual: You must be able to articulate and describe your goal to other people. When you're clear in defining your goal, and able to visualize your goal vividly, the easier it will be to determine what tasks come next. It will also be easier for other people to visualize your goal and determine if they can help you achieve your goal. Specificity is your friend.

Be Measurable: You must be able to track your progress. Giving yourself milestones along the way to your goal is key. If the goal is to "sign with a good legit agent who believes in me," how do you measure that? Completing The Savvy Mailings Plan to 20 agents or paying to meet six agents could be a measurable milestone to achieving that goal.

Be Attainable: If a goal is definable and measurable it automatically feels more attainable. "Open a checking account with Chase and maintain a minimum balance of $500" feels more attainable than "Be more responsible with money." Be aware of unrealistic goals. The odds of starring in a feature film next year as a non-union beginner are small – but a supporting role in an independent film, or three student films, could be a very attainable goal. Think big – yes. That's why we have you create your 20 Year Plan, but be realistic for your level of craft and where you're currently at in the industry.

Be Aligned: Every goal you set for yourself must be consistent with the values, beliefs, and desires you have for your life. A goal shouldn't be what you feel you 'should' do – it must be what you truly want. Remember the Be, Do, Have exercise. If film is your passion and you live in New York City, where there are a lot of opportunities in musical theater, there is no reason to feel you should learn how to sing. Align your goals with your passion.

Career Goal

In choosing your career goals, aim high. Also keep in mind that goals take time to come to fruition. Remember, this is a process. Refer back to the Career Goals Analysis Table and ask yourself these questions:

* Is there a consistency in my priorities and goals? If not, maybe that's a goal for next year.

* Is this what I really want?

* Is this a big enough goal for a year? Is it too big?

Career Goals

Write your two Career Goals in the space below. Make sure that they are worded in a way that excites you. **Remember:** When you hit one of your goals, replace it with another. Decide what you really want and have your other goals waiting in the wings.

Career Goal 1: (Transfer to page 33)

Career Goal 2: (Transfer to page 34)

Life & Financial Goals

Now choose a Life Goal and a Financial Goal and write them in the space below. If you're stuck, you can use our examples as a reference.

Life Goal: (Transfer to page 36)

Financial Goal: (Transfer to page 38)

Now transfer these four goals to the top of each of the corresponding goal worksheets.
They are labeled – Career, Life, and Financial. Put one goal in the top center of each sheet. Refer to our examples for help.

Savvy Coaching

If you are having trouble choosing your four goals, contact us. We'll set you up with one of our amazing coaches to help guide you through the process.

Visit our website at **www.thesavvyactor.com** or call **212-502-0908** to set up a one on one coaching session. And, yes, we also offer phone sessions.

Projects and Tasks

You've chosen your goals, now it's time to break them down into your projects and then tasks. Remember, a goal is the culmination of projects, and projects are a series of tasks.

To make it easier (and clearer) to break down goals, we put projects into *project categories*. These categories will help focus your projects and their related tasks into key areas, thereby making them more specific. The more specific you are, the more you will realize the attainability of your dreams.

"A journey of a thousand miles begins with a single step," according to Lao-Tzu. This kind of non-artistic planning may seem rigid to you now, but it will save you thousands of steps and guide you from taking any wrong or unhelpful detours in your life or career.

For your two Career Goals, we've already created the *project categories* for maximum effectiveness:

- **Business Materials** – What materials do I need to achieve this goal?

- **Building Relationships** – What relationships can I build to help hit this goal?

- **Defining Events** – What events need to happen to attain this goal?

With these key project categories, you can begin brainstorming all the possible projects for each category. For example, "create website" is a project within the larger project category Business Materials. As you continue brainstorming, also think in terms of actionable steps or as we refer to them, tasks. What are the things you can physically do to complete a project? We'll deal more with organizing tasks and your task list soon.

The important thing is to write down every possible project and task you can think of, because there are many ways to achieve the goals you want. If you figure out all the possibilities when you brainstorm, you can pick the most effective way to get there for you. Remember the 20 Year Plan roadmap example. There are lots of ways to drive to LA from NY. You may choose to visit your aunt in Texas first, see the giant ball of twine in Kansas or pick up a friend at Burning Man, then end in LA. As long as you have a good map and are clear about your particular path, the journey becomes your own route to success.

Creating Projects and Tasks

Now it's your turn. Use your goal worksheets to start brainstorming.

Career Projects & Tasks Exercise

1. Spend the next 20-30 minutes to brainstorm all the possible Projects and Tasks for you to achieve your two Career Goals on the following goal worksheets.

Life Projects & Tasks Exercise

1. Create your project categories for your Life Goal. Use our examples as a reference.

2. Spend the next 20-30 minutes and brainstorm all the possible Projects and Tasks for you to achieve your Life Goal on the following goal worksheets.

Financial Projects & Tasks Exercise

1. Create your project categories for your Financial Goal. Use our examples as a reference.

2. Spend the next 20-30 minutes and brainstorm all the possible Projects and Tasks for you to achieve your Financial Goal on the following goal worksheets.

Career Goal Example

Sign with a Good Legit Agent Who Believes in Me

Business Materials

Business Materials
Postcards
Business Cards
Thank You Cards
Headshot
Resume
Postage
Cover Letter
9x12 Envelopes
Labels
Press Kit
Monologue
Song Book

Building Relationships

Building Relationships
Research Savvy Mailings Plan
Create a Targeted Mailing List of Agents
Buy List Of Agents (Savvy Mailing List or other)
Find Personal Connection/Introduction To Agents
Casting Directors To Target
Research Agencies
Social Networking Sites
Research Networking Facilities - One On One, Breakthrough, The Network, Actors Connection
Research Auditions - Backstage/Actors Access
Research Agencies - Commercial/Legit, Size, Location, Reputation
Send Postcard Before Meeting
Advantages: One Night Meeting with a Casting Director vs. Class Over Several Weeks
Research CD/Agent You Are Meeting
Contact Writers, Directors, Casting Directors, Musical Directors, Composers, Accompanists, Producers, etc.

Defining Events

Defining Events
Budget
Audition Regularly
Send Thank You Card After Meetings/Auditions
Create Press Kit
Prep For Interviews
Sign Up For Savvy Mailings Webinar
Open Mics: Singing/Stand Up
Play Reading Series
You Tube: Post Content
Create/Produce Your Own Material
Class with a Casting Director
Organize A Scene Night For Industry
Vocal/Monologue Coaching
Classes w/Well Known and Respected Teachers
Research Upcoming Theater, TV Shows, and Film

Career Goal

Business Materials

Building Relationships

Defining Events

Career Goal

Business Materials

Building Relationships

Defining Events

Goals • Projects • Tasks

Life Goal Example

Achieve Balance in My Life: Focusing on Body, Mind & Spirit

Project Category 1	Project Category 2	Project Category 3
Create Healthy Habits For My Body	**Spend More Time w/Family & Friends**	**Me Time**
Workout 4 x A Week (Include Yoga)	Schedule Date Night 1 x Week	Plan A Vacation
Stretch Daily	Schedule Coffee w/Friends 1 x Week	Go To The Movies Alone 1 x Month
Take Vitamins Daily	Call Parents 2 x Week	Meditate 10 Minutes A Day
Cook Dinner At Home (To Eat Better and Cheaper)	Send Birthday Cards To Friends & Family	Read The Sunday Newspaper w/Coffee
Try Something New At Least Once A Week	Make Time Everyday To Connect With Significant Other	Read A Good Book
Shut Computer Off At 10 pm	Schedule Dinner with Friends 2 x Month	Eat A Fabulous Healthy/Unhealthy Breakfast On Sundays
Drink Decaf Coffee	Visit w/Family Every Other Month	Go To The Park 1 x Week
Find A Good Massage Therapist	Have A Boys/Girls Night Out	Splurge On A Massage, Facial, Or Personal Trainer
	Theater Date w/Friends 1 x Month	Take Dog to Park 3 x Week
		Learn Italian
		Schedule A Day To Do Nothing 1 x Month

Goals • Projects • Tasks

Life Goal

Project Category 1

Project Category 2

Project Category 3

Goals • Projects • Tasks

Start My Road to Financial Freedom by Organizing, Investing and Gaining Knowledge

Project Category 1

Organize My Finances

- Use Savvy Actor Tracking Sheets
- Write Down All Monthly Bills
- Create Receipt Filing System
- Create My Weekly Budget
- Get A New Credit Card Just For Acting Career
- File Receipts Weekly
- Purchase Quicken

Project Category 2

Figure Out My Investment Strategies For Retirement

- Research The Different Types Of IRA's
- Open An IRA
- Get Credit Report Copy - annualcreditreport.com
- Research Investing Basics
- Pay Myself First - 10%
- Research Lifecycle Funds
- Save Additional $50 A Month
- Pay Off Credit Card With Highest APR First

Project Category 3

Expand My Financial Knowledge

- Read *Secrets of the Millionaire Mind* by T. Harv Eker
- Read *Cash Machine For Life* by Loral Langemeier
- Talk w/An Accountant
- Read *Naked Economics* by Charles Wheelan
- Listen To NPR's Planet Money Podcast
- Read *Rich Dad, Poor Dad* by Robert Kiyosaki

Goals • Projects • Tasks

Financial Goal

Project Category 1

Project Category 2

Project Category 3

Goals • Projects • Tasks

Year Mapping Instructions

You have your four goals. You brainstormed your projects and tasks that need to happen to achieve each goal. Now it's time to start mapping out when things will occur. It's one thing to have goal sheets and it's another thing to incorporate them in your life.

Project Mapping Example: Getting New Headshots

Getting new headshots would be under the project category Business Materials toward your goal of getting an agent. Here is an example of how to map out the various tasks associated with this project.

January 1 – Start saving $50 a week (You will have saved $650 by your March 27 shoot)

January 27 – Research photographers (Give yourself a week or two to meet photographers)

February 1 – Call photographers to set up interviews (Give yourself a month to decide)

March 10 – Deadline to schedule photo shoot (Headshot availability varies)

March 27 – Headshot session

April 10 – Headshots picked and reproduced (You'll need about a week or two to decide.)

Get Started Mapping

Now it's your turn. You saw the example above. Use the following worksheets to map out your year. Whatever you can assign a date to, assign a date. You'll be tempted to put everything in the first quarter. But think strategically and be honest about when things could actually occur during the year. Certain things you won't be able to put a date on yet, that's okay. Don't forget to schedule around vacations, holidays, and other occasions.

Year Map: 1st Quarter

January	Date	February	Date	March	Date

Goals • Projects • Tasks

Year Map: 2nd Quarter

April	Date	May	Date	June	Date

Goals • Projects • Tasks

Year Map: 3rd Quarter

July	Date	August	Date	September	Date

Goals • Projects • Tasks

Year Map: 4th Quarter

October	Date	November	Date	December	Date

Goals • Projects • Tasks

Incorporate your Calendar

Once everything is thought out on the mapping worksheets, then you need to place those projects or tasks with specific dates in your calendar system. Whether you use a planner, Outlook, iCal, Entourage, Palm software, Google calendar, etc. – it is vital to translate your map to your calendar.

Create a system that works for you. Remember this is something you will need to practice daily to incorporate into your business.

Getting New Headshots Example (from page 39)

January

Sunday	Monday	Tuesday	Wednesday	Thursday	Friday	Saturday
					1 SAVE $50	2
3	4	5	6	7	8 SAVE $50	9
10	11	12	13	14	15 SAVE $50	16
17	18	19	20	21	22 SAVE $50	23
24/31	25	26	27	28 Research Photographers	29 SAVE $50	30

February

Sunday	Monday	Tuesday	Wednesday	Thursday	Friday	Saturday
	1 Call Photographers	2	3	4	5 SAVE $50	6
7	8	9	10	11	12 SAVE $50	13
14	15	16	17	18	19 SAVE $50	20
21	22	23	24	25	26 SAVE $50	27
28						

March

Sunday	Monday	Tuesday	Wednesday	Thursday	Friday	Saturday
	1	2	3	4	5 SAVE $50	6
7	8	9	10 Schedule Photo Shoot	11	12 SAVE $50	13
14	15	16	17	18	19 SAVE $50	20
21	22	23	24	25	26 SAVE $50	27 Headshot Session
28	29	30	31			

April

Sunday	Monday	Tuesday	Wednesday	Thursday	Friday	Saturday
				1	2	3
4	5	6	7	8	9	10 Headshots Chosen & Reproduced
11	12	13	14	15	16	17
18	19	20	21	22	23	24
25	26	27	28	29	30	

Savvy Tip

We highly recommend a computerized calendar like iCal and Outlook. They are simple to use and let you implement a color-coding system. Color-coding is a great visual reference to what you have going on in any given week. You can see at a glance where your time is being spent. Visual is memorable. For example:

Acting – Red   Personal – Blue   Day Job – Green   Health/Fitness - Purple

Categorized Task List Instructions

Once you've transferred everything into your calendar, there will be several things left over that you won't be able to assign a date. Having a long to-do list really isn't ideal. Time is wasted as you comb through your list in search of a task to do. By compartmentalizing your tasks, you will work faster and be more efficient.

Compartmentalizing your tasks is simply grouping tasks into like categories. Think in terms of context: associate each task with the location in which it needs to be completed or the type of task it is. The result is a task system that's organized for maximum speed in an actor's busy day.

Here are the basic categories you can use to group your tasks:

1. **Mac or PC** – All tasks that need to be done on your computer.
2. **Phone** – All tasks that need to be done on the phone – calls, emails, etc.
3. **Errands** – All tasks that are errands.
4. **Save for Later** (SFL)– All tasks or projects that will happen someday but not sure when. (This can be broken down into subcategories as well – *SFL: Songs to Sing*, *SFL: Classes*, *SFL: Movies to See*, *etc.*)
5. **On Hold** – All tasks/projects that are waiting on a response from another person before moving forward. We tend to put emails and calls out in the world and then forget about them.
6. **Projects** – All projects that require a series of tasks. (You can subdivide this into Personal and Acting Projects.)

Find categories that work for you. Perhaps you have the ability to get a lot done at your day job; make **Day Job** a category. Or if you get a lot of work done in your home office, make **Home Office** a category. Find what categories make sense for you.

Other categories that might be helpful are:

- **Person's Name** – All tasks associated with a particular person; spouse, family member, business partner, etc.
- **Home** – All tasks that need to be done at your home.
- **Online** – All tasks that need an internet connection.

The possibilities are endless. And empowering.

Go back through your Goal sheets and Year Mapping sheets. Take your tasks and place them in their appropriate task category. *See our Categorized Task List Example as a reference.*

Transfer all your tasks into a system. Whether it's creating an Excel spreadsheet, a Word document, using Outlook tasks, or a great software application for Mac called Things (which we love!) – we urge you to find a system to keep track of all your tasks.

Categorized Task List Example

Projects	Mac/PC	Phone
Reel	Revamp Resume With Brand In Mind	Call Reproductions To Order 200 Headshots
Social Networking Revamp	Research Send Out Cards For Mailings	Call Voice Teacher To Schedule Lesson
Build Songbook	Write Cover Letter	Call 3 Companies To Price Out Reel
Find A Financial Advisor	Set Up iPerform To Organize Auditions	Call Mom & Dad
Plan Vacation	Untag Myself From Facebook Photos	Invite Doug & Shawn To Dinner
Pay Off Highest APR Credit Card	Set Up Online Banking	Call Financial Planner
	Find A Recipe For A Breakfast Casserole	
	Pay More Than The Minimum On Credit Card	
	Research Frequent Flyer Mile Credit Cards	
	Order *Secrets Of The Millionaire Mind*	

Errands	On Hold	Save For Later
Staples: Buy 9x12 Envelopes For Headshot Mailings	DVD For Reel From Production Company	Take Bob Krakower's Class
Post Office: Buy Stamps For Headshot Mailings	Response From Monologue Coach	Take Jonathan Strauss's Class
Banana Republic: Buy New Audition Outfit	Erica Re: Coffee On Thursday	Write A Sketch To Film & Post On YouTube
GNC: Pick Up Vitamins	Check From Apple Commercial	New Desk Chair
Best Buy: Purchase Quicken	Sides For Friday's Audition	Own My Own Apartment
Join Equinox		
Actors FCU: Deposit Checks		

Categorized Task List

Projects	Mac/PC	Phone

Errands	On Hold	Save For Later

Goals • Projects • Tasks

Now that you have everything in place, the "Year Plan Overview" is your opportunity to see the year you've mapped out at a glance. It's an eagle eye view, an opportunity for you to see how you've balanced out your year.

Write down your career, life, and financial projects. Then put an X in the month that you have scheduled them. The goal is to make sure that you're not doing too much or too little in a given month. If certain months are overloaded with X's, maybe you can push a project up or push it back.

Be sure to take account of busy seasons or times you may have to work a money job. The holidays are a good time to focus on saving money because it's a good time to make money. Summer is when many professional actors work in summer stock theaters. September/October and February/March tend to be big audition seasons. When will you take vacation? Are you in a professional training program with its own demands? You need to remember those things and take them into account when you plan.

Once you've done this, take a moment to appreciate what you've accomplished. Do your goals suddenly seem more doable? Are you a little scared and/or excited? Congratulations, you've planned the work, now you can work the plan.

Career Plan Overview

	Jan	Feb	Mar	April	May	June	July	Aug	Sept	Oct	Nov	Dec
Marketing												
Classes												
Performing												
Enriching Support System												
Vacation												
Making $$$												

Goals • Projects • Tasks

Section 3:
Branding

Branding

You may read or hear the term "marketing for actors" a lot. But before you can begin to market yourself to the industry you need to understand and embrace your brand. Branding is the piece of the marketing puzzle that most actors and acting teachers leave out. Your job as an actor is to fully understand what you're selling. **In order to market yourself effectively you need to understand branding.**

Branding: (Definition from TheBusinessDirector.com)

The entire process involved in creating a unique name and image for a product (good or service) in the consumers' mind, through advertising campaigns with a consistent theme. Branding aims to establish a significant and differentiated presence in the market that attracts and retains loyal customers.

So what is branding for an actor?

Branding is your essence. It is who you are no matter if you're hanging out with your friends, auditioning, meeting an agent, or at a party – it's the constant that you always bring with you.

The brand is where you get to really empower yourself. Instead of trying to be all things to all people, it's about being be who you authentically are and reflecting it in every aspect of how you present yourself. Actors tend to give their power away. Instead of owning who they are, they try to fit a mold.

When crafting your brand, you need to focus on your unique characteristics. Keep in mind that everything you do shapes your personal brand - your language, your appearance, your behavior, etc. Start with your strengths because they make you unique. Ask yourself the following questions:

- Where exactly do I fit in the theatrical world?
- What TV shows are out there that I can do right now?
- What film genre suits me best?
- Where do I fit in the commercial world?
- What shows are out there that I could be cast in right now? (not five years from now)

The point is you need to get specific and fully embrace your essence, your bread and butter. If you aren't branding yourself, others are branding you.

Brand Promise:

A brand is a promise to the decision makers in the business. For actors it's crucial to carry through on their promise, from the initial headshot, to the follow up, to getting in the door. Consistency will fulfill that promise. Create your brand with your strengths and unique characteristics in mind.

---

5 Essential Brand Characteristics

Agents and casting directors need an entry point to understanding what you offer. The more specific and perceptive you are about yourself, the better people in the business will understand how to begin a relationship with you. There are five components that will guide you in crafting your brand. These pieces will help you discover what is unique about you – what you are essentially promoting about yourself.

1.Type

Type is the starting point in crafting your brand and beginning those relationships. Embracing your type is the key to this business and getting your foot in the door. Type can carry certain preconceived notions or emotional connections for actors, especially when terms like *character actor* or *ingénue* are used. Nobody wants to be pigeon-holed.

Character is really your essence. It can be quirky, dark, gothic, bubbly, scary, arrogant, or bitchy. You need to know what kind of character you are. When you look at casting notices you'll see roles described as 'a Katie Holmes type,' 'a Matthew Broderick type,' or 'a Nicole Kidman type.' You get immediate images and an understanding of how they're trying to cast the project. Using these mental shortcuts, you can communicate your brand or type. In musical theater, your vocal range also helps to communicate type.

2. Personality

You can't deny your energy. You walk in the room with it whether you want to or not. What we're really talking about is your essence. It's that energy that differentiates you from someone else.

3. Perception

Everyone has their own perception of themselves. But it's important to do the research to know how others perceive you, because that's how you'll be cast at first. This business is subjective. Not everyone will see the same thing. But it's important to know how the majority of people view you. And don't forget, how you handle yourself professionally in this business is also a part of the industry's perception.

4. Style

Your image and personal style (clothes, hair, etc.) are important pieces of your brand. Remember, in this business, as in life, we are constantly making impressions. If someone shows up at an audition wearing a polka dot dress or tie, subliminally you'd think they're fun, bubbly, maybe offbeat. Your sense of style helps with the mental shortcuts.

5. Career Goals

It's your passion that will drive you and give you longevity in this business. Your career goals need to be included when crafting your brand because your commercial brand (on camera and print) might be slightly different than your legit brand (theater, film, TV, musical theater).

Basic Type Breakdown

Adapted from Brian Blythe's Musical Theater Type Breakdown
(Associate Artistic Director at The York Theatre, NYC)

Female Types	Age Range	Look
Ingénue	Teens- 20's	Beautiful
Character Sidekick	Teens- 20's	Unique, funny, offbeat
Leading Lady	20's-40's	Beautiful
Character Woman	30's-50's	Unique, funny, offbeat
Older Leading Lady	40+	Varies
Ensemble	Varies	Varies

Male Types	Age Range	Look
Ingénue	Teens- 20's	Handsome
Character Sidekick	Teens- 50's	Unique, funny, offbeat
Leading Man	20's-50's	Dashing, handsome
Character Leading Man	30's-50's	Unique, funny, offbeat
Ensemble	Varies	Varies

What Type Are You?

Now It's Time To Get Creative And Craft Your Brand!

1. Fill in the Personal Brand Breakdown worksheet.

2. Email 10-20 friends, family members, casting directors, or directors you've worked with and have them answer questions 6 & 7 on the Personal Brand Breakdown worksheet.

3. Once you've received the responses from your email move on to the Brand Analysis.

Personal Brand Breakdown

1. What kinds of roles do you get cast in? What's the description of those roles, the essence? (innocent girl next door, urban edgy guy, geeky underdog, etc.)

2. What kinds of roles do you want to play? (serious intelligent women, goofy nerdy men, etc.)

3. What are your strengths as a performer?

4. What are you strengths as a person?

5. How do you want to make people feel when you perform?

6. List 10 – 20 adjectives that describe you. Preferably how others have described you, such as casting directors, directors, teachers, friends – things you hear over and over again.

7. List at least 10 celebrities you get compared to that play the kinds of roles you get cast in and want to play.

8. When crafting your brand we like to look to outside sources to get a different perspective. Now it's time to think outside the box. What kind of soap are you? Think about color, smell, type of use. *(Are you a lavender French soap, Dove body wash with bursting beads, a rich exfoliator, a fruity bubble bath?)*

Brand Analysis

Once you get all the branding questions answered from your family and friends, it's time to analyze all the information about how you're perceived.

1. First read through all the information three or four times. Become familiar with it. Notice the similarities versus which descriptive words aren't repeated as much.

2. Next using the Brand Tally Sheet, begin to look for your three overall essences. Start to group similar adjectives in terms of the essences you project. Think in terms of Mind (Intellect), Body (Presence), Spirit (Soul). This will help you create a three dimensional Brand.
   Remember: Essence is who you are at your core, what makes you you, what makes you unique, what makes people respond to you.

3. Once your three overall essences are determined, start placing the names of the celebrities you got (that you like and connect with) in the essence category that makes sense for that person.

   Tip: When dealing with celebrities, it is not just about whom you resemble physically. It's those celebrities that play the kinds of roles you get cast in or want to get cast in, and who embody those adjectives that are on your list.

4. Now that the celebrities are in an essence category, narrow it down to one celebrity in each category that you feel fits you the best.

5. Finally, craft your Branding Statement on the worksheet provided. The Branding Statement is a tag line, a one sentence description of you and your essence – your product.

Branding Statement examples:

- *Imagine the California cool of Owen Wilson fused with the zany physical comedy of Jim Carrey – that's me.*

- *I'm the female Steve Buscemi.*

- *I have a bohemian spirit - with a bit of Reese Witherspoon's bubbly spark and a dash of the fearless spontaneity of Drew Barrymore.*

- *I've got the charm & charisma of a Hugh Jackman, the brooding anger of a Christian Bale, and the genuine honesty of a young Anthony Hopkins.*

- *Think Mary Louise Parker meets Rachel Griffiths meets a little bit of Kate Beckinsale and you've got me.*

Branding is a process. Try out your statement. Live with it. Tell people. See how it fits. Play with the structure, the format and each descriptive until it fits you like a glove. The words you choose need to reflect your brand as well. Reese Witherspoon would not use the same words to sell her product as Hugh Jackman or Steve Buscemi.

Brand Tally Sheet

Mind (Intellect) Essence 1	Body (Presence) Essence 2	Spirit (Soul) Essence 3
Celebrities	**Celebrities**	**Celebrities**

Use the space below to brainstorm and craft your Branding Statement.

Section 4:
Marketing

The key to this business is understanding, crafting, and embracing your brand, then consistently marketing that brand. Marketing never stops. Once you get an agent it doesn't stop. Once you get on Broadway, a soap, a sitcom, or a film – it doesn't stop.

We hear the term marketing all the time, but what does that mean for an actor? To help you better understand, we've created our own Savvy Definition of Marketing targeted for performers.

Savvy Definition of Marketing

Marketing is the creative promotion of your **essence, relationships, and successes.**

Every piece of marketing you send out, whether it be a cover letter, postcard, thank you card, show invite, reel, etc., must contain two of the three pieces of our marketing definition.

1. **Essence** – Your brand.

2. **Relationships** – Who you know, who you've auditioned for, known teachers, etc.

3. **Successes** – Bookings, callbacks, readings, shows, great classes, etc.

Everything you do to promote yourself, and your career, is encompassed under marketing and you need to create specific strategies for your goals and brand.

How do you create marketing strategies that work?

Consistency is Key. You MUST have consistency in your marketing that encompasses everything - follow up, mailings, audition material, interviews, etc. Those you are auditioning for and marketing to will trust in you, your brand and your small business because what they see on paper is always who comes in the door.

A common problem among actors when they attempt to market themselves is that they are not specific in their marketing. They send two or three different headshots. What they're selling, their brand, gets muddled. As a result, the messages they send become confusing.

It's important to remember that casting directors, directors and agents are the consumers. When you decide on your brand, it's important that you reach out to them with consistency across everything you do. Everything associated with your business should have a common theme or feeling to it. For example, everything **The Savvy Actor** sends out has our logo and red and gray company colors.

Be consistent not only in the look and style of your various marketing materials, but also in your word choice and tone from your cover letters to your website. How do you want people to know you? How do you want people to remember you?

Your marketing materials MUST support and reflect your brand, even down to the fonts on your resume. Below is a list of materials that should reflect you and be consistent with each other as a whole:

- Audition Material
- Headshot
- Resume
- Cover letter
- Business cards
- Postcards
- Thank You Cards
- Press Kit
- Social Networking Sites
- Website
- Reels/Demos
- Bio
- Newsletter
- Reviews
- Testimonials

Your audition material has to reflect what you're selling. You may like a particular piece, but if it doesn't reflect your brand, you are doing yourself a disservice.

Use the space below to list your current audition material. Examine each audition piece and ask yourself the following questions:

- Does it reflect my brand?
- What is my reason for choosing the particular piece?
- Do I love it?

Monologues

Songs

Commercial Copy

Sides

Headshot

Your headshot is your company logo. It needs to scream your essence. Your picture must be an authentic representation of you and your brand. In terms of creating consistency for your business, your marketing strategy must include the same image on your postcard, business cards, and thank you cards.

Headshots can range anywhere from $200-$1100. The most important thing is that it looks like a professional photograph. Your headshot is your first impression. If it's an amateur-looking shot, you will come across as an amateur actor. It's important to have headshots that reflect the industry standard. Up until 2005 in NYC, black and white was the standard. Now your headshot must be in color or you'll seem out of date.

Photo Shoot

Once you find a photographer whose work you like and you've interviewed, it's time to start prepping for your photo shoot. Selecting clothes and colors that look best on you and are indicative of your brand is essential to an effective shoot. We urge you to take photos of yourself in the clothes before the day of the shoot, because clothes may photograph much differently than they look in the mirror.

Ladies, you should have a makeup artist for your photo shoot. Your hair and make up should look like you on your best day, not after $150 worth of make-up and hair styling that's impossible to recreate on your own.

Bottom line, nothing should distract from you and your eyes. During the shoot, think natural and open and warm. Draw us in. Also keep your brand in mind as you're taking pictures so they're an accurate representation of you and what you sell.

Picking Your Headshots

When you get your proofs, narrow them down to ten to twenty and ask casting directors, directors, agents, and other actors whose opinions you respect to pick the one that best reflects your brand. Refer back to your Branding Statement to help you narrow down your choice.

We've found that the best shot is not always the one you, your parents, or your significant other like the best. They have their own image of you and it may not reflect your professional brand. They know the comfortable you, not the first impression you.

Your headshot can either be a horizontal or vertical shot, a three quarter shot, or a tight headshot. Whatever showcases you best and reflects your brand. This is a subjective business. Each person will have their own opinions on what style they like best. Most importantly, be careful with retouching. All digital headshots must be retouched, but people tend to overdo it and end up with a shot that looks fake.

You may use a different headshot for commercial work (on-camera and print) than you do for legit work (theater, musical theater, TV, Film).

Resumes

Resumes are an integral marketing tool for actors. Your resume needs to reflect your brand and where you are in the business. And remember, it will change regularly.

First and foremost, make sure your resume is clear, legible, and honest. Don't lie, you will get caught. Make sure to keep your resume up to date and current. Do not put your address, age, or measurements.

Resumes help the industry know who you are and what you do. There's no need to put every show you've ever done. The roles should be a representation of you and your brand. If you're just out of school without many credits, training is the most important thing. As you gain more professional experience, those college credits will slowly go away.

Fonts and Colors

Fonts and colors are used to create a mood and guide people to the information you want them to see. Fonts selection will give the reader a feel for you. There are comic fonts, bold-intense fonts, sweet fonts, simple fonts, fun fonts. What type of font reflects what you're selling?

Color is used to highlight your resume. Keep it simple. Use one color or at most two. Keep in mind that whatever color(s) you choose also needs to reflect your brand. (Refer back to the soap question on the Personal Brand Breakdown Exercise for ideas.)

While we urge our clients to think outside of the box with their marketing tools, there are industry standards that should be followed. That's why we created the Resume Outline Worksheet to jot down your info in the appropriate categories and start you on the right path.

Theater Categorization

When first starting out, you will use all your credits, but as you advance in your career and book more roles, you will be able to be more selective on the roles you use to represent your work. Organize your resume, by best credits. Broadway, Tours, Regional. Then by role. You may use the name of the character.

Film Role Categorization

In film and television, character names do not mean as much as the billing does. For film use (listed in order of importance): Lead, Supporting, Featured.

Television Role Categorization

For television use (listed in order of importance): Series Regular, Recurring, Guest Star, Co-star.

Resume Outline Worksheet

New to the Industry? Use this outline to begin.

Name		
Email		Height
Phone		Weight/Size
Website		Hair Color
Unions		Eye Color

Theater		
Show	Role	Theater/ Production Company

Film		
Show	Role	Theater/ Production Company

Training	
Class Type	Class/ Teacher

Special Skills

Jodie Bentley

Jodie Bentley

AEA AFTRA SAG

KERIN-GOLDBERG ASSOCIATES
155 East 55th Street
New York, NY 10022
212-838-7373

| Hair: Red | Eyes: Blue | Height: 5'2" | www.JodieBentley.com |

FILM & TELEVISION

One Life To Live	Recurring	ABC
Guiding Light	U/5	CBS
Employee of The Month	Lead	Sedagive Entertainment
April Showers	Lead	Coffee N' Cake Productions
Denis Leary's Christmas Special	Featured	Comedy Central
The World's Tallest Buildings	Featured	Discovery Channel

NEW YORK THEATRE

Captain Louie (NYC Premiere)	Various roles	The York Theatre / Meridee Stein
Cyclone & The Pig-Faced Lady	Cyclone	NYMF - TBG / Edyta Marden
Angry Young Teen-age Girl Gang	Didi	NYMF - Atlantic Stage / Mark Rounds
Next Year in Jerusalem	Faustine	WorkShop Theater / Rob McIntosh
The A-Train (re) Plays	Tanya	Peter Jay Sharp Theatre / Hope Clarke
Soundtrack To Cezanne	Summer	WorkShop Theater / Spook Testani
The Expatriates	Dorothy Parker	The Krane Theatre / Randy Anderson
The Gift of the Magi	Della	The Workshop Theatre / Kathleen Brant
Superman Is Dead	Lead (16 roles)	The Connelly Theatre / Dominic Orlando
Macabaret (MAC nomination)	Faygela	Don't Tell Mama / Rick Skye

REGIONAL THEATRE

Sylvia	Sylvia	Cortland Rep. Theatre / Joe Ametrano
Annie Get Your Gun	Annie	Shawnee Playhouse / Carmella Mayo
Prelude To A Kiss	Rita	Bristol Valley Theatre / GaryJohn LaRosa
They're Playing Our Song	Sonia	Cortland Rep. Theatre / Michael Perrosa
The Star Spangled Girl	Sophie	Fredonia Opera House / Kathy Rossetter
The Grey Zone	Girl	Downstairs Cabaret / Chris Kawalsky
Pump Boys and Dinettes	Rhetta	Bristol Valley Theatre / Keith Andrews
The Story of Anne Frank	Miep	Dandelion Productions / Dan Carmello
Godspell	Robin	Bristol Valley Theatre / Keith Andrews
Have A Nice Day	Ronda	Downstairs Cabaret / Rick Lewis

COMMERCIAL
Conflicts for National and Regional On-Camera and Radio Commercials available upon request.

TRAINING

Acting:	BFA; NYU, Tisch School of the Arts, Stella Adler Conservatory:
	Alice Winston, Robert Perillo, James Tripp, Nicholas Kepros, Tom Oppenheim
Voice:	Andrew Byrne, Jeff Buchsbaum, Ells Stone, Alix Korey
Musical Theatre:	VP Boyle, Dave Clemmons, Richard Sabellico, Jamibeth Margolis, Sheri Sanders (pop/rock)
Dance:	Broadway Dance: Jazz, Basic Tap
Commercial:	Doreen Frumkin, Colleen Patrick
Advanced Film/TV:	Pat McCorkle, Victoria Visgilio, Jonathan Strauss, Christine Kromer
Musical Improv:	Brian Blythe, Tammy Holder

SPECIAL SKILLS
Sight Reading, Basic Baton Twirling, Yoga, Pilates, Aerobics, Running, Various Dialects (great ear), Voice-Overs, Great with dogs and kids, Home Decorating, Co-Owner of The Savvy Actor

Savvy Resume Guide

Want to have a resume that reflects your brand but don't know how to start?
We've created a step-by-step resume guide to help you create your own unique resume using Microsoft Word. Works for Mac and PC.

Visit our Website at **www.thesavvyactor.com** to learn more.

Cover Letter

Once your branding statement is crafted, it's time to put it to use to create a strong cover letter. A cover letter must be included with every headshot you mail. It serves as your first introduction to many agent and casting director's offices. Cover letters are an excellent marketing tool and a great way to promote you and your brand.

A cover letter should be reflective of who you are, what you offer, and be written in your voice – not a formal tone. Acting is a business, and you need to treat it as one. However, a formal cover letter doesn't work in this business because they're too long, too dry, or sound like a laundry list of accomplishments. You already have a better list of your accomplishments – your resume!

Be personable and write as if to your peers – not an authority figure. We're all peers in this business; actors, casting directors, agents, directors, etc. We just have different responsibilities within the industry. Industry people are incredibly busy, which is why we believe **cover letters should be three sentences**. Any longer and the recipient won't read it – they don't have time. This will keep you from writing that boring laundry list of successes, which doesn't showcase your personality anyway. Short, sweet and to the point is respected in any industry. Especially ours.

Three Sentences of a Cover Letter (The sentences can be in any order.)

1st sentence = Branding statement

2nd sentence = Relationship or success *(refer back to our Savvy Definition of Marketing)*

3rd sentence = Asking for what you want.

Sign-Offs

Typical letter sign-offs (All the Best, Sincerely, Warm Regards, Yours Truly) are too formal for this business. Instead create your own sign-off. It lets the recipient know more about you. Be creative, be memorable and leave them with something that allows them to get who you are in an instant. **Examples** – *With Sass & Class, Spontaneously Yours, Have A Good One, etc.*

Packaging

Your headshot resume and cover letter are a package. We recommend stapling or paper-clipping your cover letter to your headshot. Keep your cover letter small and create a letterhead with your name and contact information on it. Never cover your face.

In Kevin's example: a cover letter was created by printing four to a page and then trimming to size using a paper cutter.

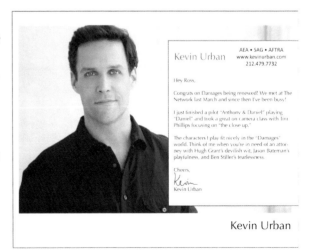

Kevin Urban

Sample Agent Cover Letter

Hi Heather,

OK, so think Sarah Jessica Parker meets Bernadette Peters meets Debra Messing ....and here I am!

I just played the sassy and carefree Faustine in **Next Year in Jerusalem** at The WorkShop Theater.   I also performed the title role of Cyclone, an impulsive chanteuse and superhero, in **Cyclone (and The Pig Faced Lady)** at the New York Musical Theatre Festival to sold out houses.

I'm in the process of setting up agency interviews and would love to add you to my list. I've heard some wonderful things about your agency and can't wait to meet you!

With Vim & Vigor,
Jodie Bentley

Write your agent cover letter below.

Sample Submission Cover Letter

Hey Ross,

Congrats on Damages being renewed! We met at The Network last March and since then I've been busy!

I just finished a pilot "Anthony & Daniel" playing "Daniel" and took a great on camera class with Tim Phillips focusing on "the close up."

The characters I play fit nicely in the "Damages" world. Think of me when you're in need of an attorney with Hugh Grant's devilish wit, Jason Bateman's playfulness, and Ben Stiller's fearlessness.

Cheers,

Kevin Urban

Write your submission cover letter below.

Postcards

Postcards are great strategic marketing tools. They're used for promoting your successes and relationships. After your headshot and resume, they are the second vehicle into an agent or casting director's office. They serve as excellent, inexpensive reminders of your logo (headshot photo) and your brand.

Your postcard must use the same photo as your headshot. By doing so you are continuing to create brand recognition. You see this all the time when the same TV commercials are repeated, sometimes within the same commercial break. Companies use these proven techniques in their marketing and so should you.

The Strategy

The nature of a postcard means that it does not have to be opened (do not put it in an envelope), and as a result anyone can see it. The more people that see it, the more bang for your buck. You're playing on human curiosity. A postcard sitting on a desk will be seen.

There's another reason to use postcards. Email inboxes of casting directors and agents have become inundated with casting notices, contracts, client correspondence and, of course, spam. One agent told us that she gets 400 emails a day. The point for any marketing is to stand out. When actors send email updates, they don't stand out, and more than likely if they don't know you, your message won't be opened. Postcards will be seen.

Postcards are small and don't take up much space. A postcard forces you to keep your message short. Like the cover letter, it should be no more than three sentences. Like all your marketing material, it should be written in your voice and promote a relationship or success.

Postcards make financial sense. They cost less to send than a headshot and resume or thank you card. They promote your logo (headshot photo), your product, and remind people of your brand. They are inexpensive billboards.

Finally, postcards will be thrown away. Come to terms with it and know you are planting the seeds for success. They will have to look at it to throw it out!

Thank You Cards

Thank you cards are an important piece in your marketing plan because you are thanking someone and not asking for anything.

The Strategy

Unlike a postcard or headshot, there is a ceremony to opening cards. People enjoy getting them and they're generally the first thing people open. Casting directors and agents are human, too. Plus, it's one piece of marketing that will definitely go directly to the person it's addressed to.

Sending a card after *every* audition or call back is a way to show gratitude in a business where actors are constantly asking for something. Remember what your mother taught you. Thank you's count.

Your headshot photo must be inside every thank you card. This will create brand recognition. If your handwriting is bad, they might not even know whom it's from without a photo.

Think of it this way. If they can't read your message, and there's no picture, you've wasted two dollars. If you've sent out ten cards, that's twenty dollars you could have used towards a class or coaching. Be smart in your strategy and always include your company logo, your headshot photo.

Again, you're not asking for anything in a thank you card – you are simply thanking the person. That doesn't mean, however, that you can't say that you will follow up with them next week or month.

You can send cards for birthdays, holidays, lots of occasions. They serve as another way to stand out from the crowd. Cards can sit on desks or shelves and serve as a reminder of you and your brand.

NOTE: Postcards are not thank you cards.

A postcard is for promoting yourself and a thank you card is for expressing gratitude to someone else. There is a difference.

Business Card

Business cards can serve as a quick reminder of you and your brand long after you've met someone. Business cards are smaller than postcards and handed out quickly and easily. They ooze professionalism.

As with all of your marketing it needs to reflect your brand. You can be creative with your business card, but the colors, fonts, and headshot should remain consistent with all your marketing. Remember, you are creating a package.

Business Card Needs To Have Your:

- Headshot
- Phone Number
- Email Address
- Website Address

Optional:

- Union Affiliation
- Press Quotes
- Branding Statement
- Double Sided Printing

At **The Savvy Actor** we don't believe in mass mailings, but rather, specific and targeted mailings. You will be marketing yourself every week, with consistency and structure. And you will see results. Check out the testimonials on our website.

The Strategy

There are three vehicles into an office when doing a mailing. We have already discussed them, but now let's look at each one's specific purpose.

1. **Headshot/Resume and Cover Letter package** – This is your first introduction to an office – your package. One that will most likely be opened up by an assistant. That's why your headshot, your cover letter and your resume must reflect your brand/essence. Your package must be creative, clean, and designed to make you stand out from the pack.

2. **Postcard** – The second vehicle into an office – your billboard. It's out in the open for all to see, an excellent reminder of your logo (headshot photo) and brand. It's the vehicle you'll be using the most.

3. **Thank You Card** – The third vehicle into the office and the most vital part of your strategy – gratitude. Actors tend to ask for a lot of things. *What do you think of my headshot? Can I get seen for that audition? Can you recommend a monologue?* By thanking others for their time, feedback, and energy, you'll come across as a thoughtful person, not a needy actor. *And best of all*, thank you cards will always be opened by the person to whom they're addressed.

Tips for Mailings:

- Create a targeted list of agents and casting directors based on your goals and your brand. (See worksheets page 75 – 77)

- Always send your mailings on a Sunday or Monday, so that they'll arrive by midweek.

- Make sure to set aside office hours every week for yourself to do your mailings.

- Always pick one person per department to target, do not target everyone at once.

- Stay consistent with your picture; it should be the same picture on your headshot, postcard, and thank you cards. We've already mentioned consistency – but it's worth repeating, you MUST be consistent with what you are putting out to the world so people get you in an instant. It's not about having a postcard with two images to show range – show them what you do best! (Keep in mind, a commercial mailing may use a different photo than a mailing to legit agents.)

Using The Savvy Mailings Plan

The Savvy Mailings Plan (see the next page) is a system to take you out of overwhelm and give you a structured approach to building relationships. Because that's what mailings are meant to do, build relationships. You'll send eight pieces of mail to each agent, four to each casting director on your targeted list. Each week has a specific and strategic objective. Some of you are probably thinking "I don't know enough casting directors to mention in my mailing to agents." This is the time to be proactive. If you don't know enough people, get yourself to an open call or pay to meet them at the various networking facilities (you can find a list of NYC networking facilities on our Resource Center at TheSavvyActor.com.) The Savvy Mailings Plan is about impressing the people on your list with your *forward momentum*. It's like creating your own buzz. The combination of the Savvy Mailings Plan and investing in specific networking seminars or classes is powerful for your career. Commit fully, play fully, and be open to success. Remember, one mailing every four months will not a career make.

Financial Breakdown

You will notice in The Savvy Mailings Plan, that we give you a financial breakdown after each week so you know how much you are spending to do your mailing. The budget is based on a mailing of ten headshots. If ten pictures are not in your budget, send five, if you can afford more, send fifteen or twenty. The important thing is to begin and begin it properly. Don't start by sending thirty pictures out and only get to Week 3 because you run out of money. Budget properly and do what you can handle financially. Be a smart businessperson all around.

Maintenance List

Once you audition or interview with someone in the industry (or you mail to an agent eight weeks in a row or a casting director four weeks in a row) – they then go on your Maintenance List. Every six to eight weeks you should send your Maintenance List a postcard of what has been going on in your business in terms of successes or relationships. You *must* remind people that you exist and what you are up to. This is a marketing investment in your career and the Maintenance List is the key to being remembered.

We already mentioned that we don't believe in mass mailings but targeted ones – that's because it's not just a numbers game. Whether you are trying to land an agent or get a casting director to know your work, it's vital to remember that building relationships is a process. We are in a business of building, creating and maintaining relationships – the Maintenance List is the catalyst to keep that going.

Your job is to nurture your relationships equally; you never know which ones will flourish.

The Savvy Mailings Plan

Action	Budget (average of 10 sent per week)
Week 1 Send 10-20 headshots/resumes to your targeted list. Include a brief cover letter attached to your picture (DO NOT cover your face.)	Headshot/Resume: $10.00 Postage: $10.50 Total Week 1: $20.50
Week 2 Send a postcard to your targeted list letting them know you sent a picture/resume last week and you are just making sure they received it.	Postcards: $6.20 Postage: $2.80 Total Week 2: $9.00
Week 3 Send another postcard to your targeted list. • Let agents know two Casting Directors (CD's) you've recently met. • Let CD's know recent successes or people who know your work.	Postcards: $6.20 Postage: $2.80 Total Week 3: $9.00
Week 4 – (Last week for Casting Directors) Send a thank you card to your targeted list with your headshot printed inside (or use a business card). Simply thank them for looking at your picture/resume *(NOTE: CD's go into your maintenance mailing sent every 6 – 8 weeks)*	Cards: $9.30 Postage: $4.40 Total Week 4: $13.70 **Total CD Mailing Cost: $52.20**
Week 5 – (Continue for Agents) Send another postcard to targeted agents describing your brand and which roles you've been cast in. Be VERY specific.	Postcards: $6.20 Postage: $2.80 Total Week 5: $9.00
Week 6 Send another postcard to targeted agents letting them know two more casting directors who you've seen recently.	Postcards: $6.20 Postage: $2.80 Total Week 6: $9.00
Week 7 Send another postcard to targeted agents including a quote from a review you got, a callback, or a booking.	Postcards: $6.20 Postage: $2.80 Total Week 7: $9.00
Week 8 – Last week For Agents Send a card to with your headshot printed inside (or use a business card) to targeted agents. Let them know you would like to meet with them and you will call them next week to set up an interview. *(Always call midweek, make the phone call after hours and leave a message. Rehearse what you are going to say and be positive!)*	Cards: $9.30 Postage: $4.40 Total Week 8: $13.70 **Total Agent Mailing Cost: $92.90**

- Headshot pricing based on Reproductions reorder of 100 Headshots at $95.60 plus tax; Postage $1.05 per envelope; Does not include copying of Resumes or 9x12 envelopes.
- Savvy Mailings Service Wholesale Postcard Price $.62; Postcard Postage $.28.
- Savvy Mailings Service Wholesale Card Price $.93; Greeting Card Postage $.44.
- The Savvy 8 Week Mailings Plan is a culmination of our own personal experience with actor mailings adapted from the teachings of Brian O'Neil and Scott Glasgow.

Sample Postcards, Thank You Cards, and Show Invites

Jodie Bentley
in
Cyclone and The Pig Faced Lady
at The Barrow Group
312 West 36th Street, 3rd Floor

Tues, Sep 23rd at 8:00 pm
Wed, Sep 24th at 1:00 pm
Sun, Sep 28th at 4:30 pm
Wed, Oct 1st at 8:00 pm
Fri, Oct 3rd at 4:30 pm
Sat, Oct 4th at 8:00 pm

www.nymf.org/Show-918.hmtl

Hi Jodie!

NYMF is here! Complete with a Coney Island freak show, vaudeville acts, a villain, and a superheroine to save the day - me! We are in the midst of rehearsals for Cyclone, and I am loving delving into the complexity of a comic book superhero, with her different personas, and finding the truth behind the style. Think Sarah Jessica Parker fused with Kim Cattrall and Bette Midler!

Since you haven't seen me do anything the commercial audition room, you to be my guest me a call on my cell tickets aside for you

Hope you had a relaxing

With Vim & Vigor,

Jodie Bentley

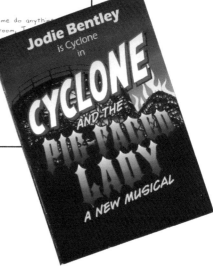

Savvy Mailings Service

The mailings plan is a breeze to set up with the Savvy Mailings Service. You'll be promoting yourself to agents and casting directors faster, smarter, easier and cheaper than you ever have before.

Check out our next FREE webinar. For details go to: **www.mailingsforactors.com**

Targeted Legit Agent List

Remember, you're running a business and must be specific in who you target. No more mass mailings. Create a list of targeted legit agents that are right for your goals and where you're at in the business.

Agency	Agent Name
1.	
2.	
3.	
4.	
5.	
6.	
7.	
8.	
9.	
10.	
11.	
12.	
13.	
14.	
15.	

Savvy Tip

Keep in mind that today's assistants are tomorrow's agents. Many agents don't have time to attend showcases and other performances. Instead, target their assistants. Assistants are often the ones who open mail and see shows. They're also who agents rely on to find "new" talent.

Remember, you're running a business and must be specific in who you target. No more mass mailings. Create a list of targeted commercial agents that are right for your goals and where you're at in the business.

Agency	Agent Name
1.	
2.	
3.	
4.	
5.	
6.	
7.	
8.	
9.	
10.	
11.	
12.	
13.	
14.	
15.	

Savvy Tip

Let your personality shine during your commercial agent interview. The commercial world is all about personality. We'll teach you how to showcase yourself and your personality later in the manual when we talk about your **30 Second Blurb**.

Targeted Casting Director List

Target specific casting directors based on your goals. For the mailings plan, choose ten casting directors. Choose only one person from each office. We've given you twenty spaces below. Use ten for commercial casting directors and ten for theater, film or TV, depending on your goals.

Casting Office	CD Name
1.	
2.	
3.	
4.	
5.	
6.	
7.	
8.	
9.	
10.	
11.	
12.	
13.	
14.	
15.	
16.	
17.	
18.	
19.	
20.	

Interviews are a powerful marketing tool. Most people wing them, but interviews need to be prepared for in advance. Give yourself time. There is an art to interviews and that art, much like crafting a role, is in the preparation.

The interview is like a first date. You're both trying to look your best and impress each other. You both have hopes that this relationship may be 'the one.' In life, we are generally attracted to confident people. When you go into a store, don't you appreciate an outgoing, knowledgeable salesperson who answers your questions without taking five minutes or beating around the bush? So will the person who's interviewing you.

Your preparation will allow you to have answers ready to the questions the agent, casting director or director will ask, without having to formulate an answer on the spot. The strategizing has been done ahead of time, and you won't walk out of the meeting thinking, "Oh! I should have said *that*."

The following sheets will lead your through your interview preparation.

Savvy Tip

We can't stress the importance of role-play. Speak your answers out loud. It's just like learning a script, the more you rehearse, the more naturally it will flow from you.

Interview Questions

The following is a list of questions that may be asked in an agent interview. Write down the main points to include in your responses, then role play the answers. Be prepared to show who you are as a person and as a brand.

1. What's your story?

2. Where are you originally from?

3. What did you do this weekend?

4. Where do you see yourself in this industry?

5. Who knows your work?

6. What shows are playing now that you fit into?

7. What brought you to NYC, LA, etc.?

8. So what's next?

9. What project did you enjoy the most and why?

10. What have you been up to lately?

11. Do you have any questions for me?

12. Who are you freelancing with?

13. What other agents have you met?
(You don't have to tell an agent the other agents you've met, but you do have to have a response to this question.)

Imagine walking into an agent's office with a packet that answers all their questions in advance. Think of the confidence you'll feel and how impressed they'll be. Confidence is sexy. Understanding the acting business is sexy. Agents want to work with people who know who they are and who are confident about their brand. The Savvy Press Kit does just that.

The Savvy Press Kit is a powerful marketing tool that allows a legit agent to know exactly where you see yourself in the industry. It's a tool to help them sell you.

A commercial agent's needs are much simpler: give them a list of commercial casting directors who know you.

The following worksheets will guide you in creating your Savvy Press Kit.

1. **Create a list of casting directors, directors, artistic directors, etc., who know your work.**
    (Those people that, if an agent called, would know you and your work.)

2. **Create a list of the theater projects you are right for.**
    (Current and Upcoming Broadway/ Off Broadway Shows/Regional)

3. **Create a list of the TV shows that you are right for.**
   (Current and Upcoming Shows)

4. **Create a list of Film Directors, Producers, Script Writers who typically are associated with projects that excite you and that are right for your brand.**
   (*For Example* - James Cameron's projects are typically big budget action movies)

5. **Create a list of "outside the box" roles.**
   (Roles that you love that go against your type)

6. **Compile your reviews on a separate page.**

This is one example of how you can format your Press Kit. The possibilities are endless. Be creative!

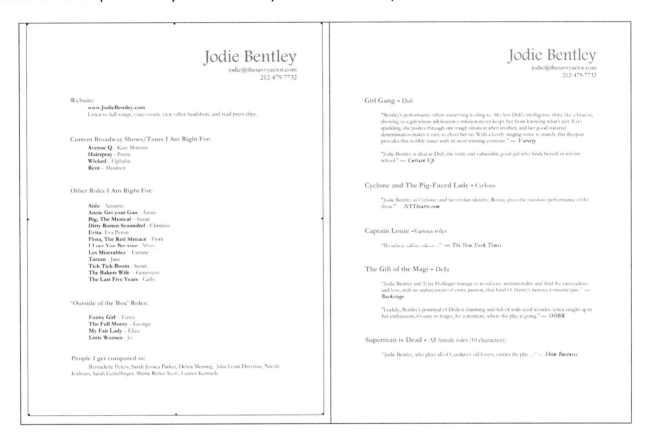

The Savvy Press Kit Package

Your Savvy Press Kit must be packaged. Use a folder or other type of material. You can be creative with your packaging. Remember to incorporate your brand colors and fonts.

The examples on this page are for reference. If you are at the beginning of your career, start with one page. As your career expands, so will your Savvy Press Kit.

30 Second Blurb

The 30 Second Blurb is the answer to, "So tell me about yourself." It's a question that always comes up in an interview.

Many actors think, "I'll just be myself and wing it." They don't anticipate the adrenaline, the nerves, the excitement, and the desire to please. In hindsight they desperately wish they'd been better prepared. Like everything else in this manual, the 30 Second Blurb must be crafted. It will be a marketing tool you'll need in almost any setting. That's why it's vital to have an answer scripted and prepared. Use it to effectively showcase your personality and your business savvy.

Leave your response open ended, or end it with a question. Remember, an interview is a dialogue.

Here are some tips when creating your blurb:

1. **Points of Reference/Structure**
    a. A bit about your past/personal life (you don't have to start with where you're from)
    b. Where you're at now professionally and what you're looking for
    c. What you are passionate about
    d. What you want

2. **Things to Include**
    a. Your strengths
    b. Your personality
    c. Your brand
    d. What you do best
    e. What makes you different/stand out
    f. Where you're most marketable

       (Theater, musical theater, commercial, film, TV, etc.)

3. **When you're done, ask yourself**
    a. Does it represent you?
    b. Does it represent your brand?

Write your 30 Second Blurb below.

Savvy **Phone Coaching**

Need help crafting your 30 Second Blurb? Contact us. We'll set you up with a coach to guide you and help you role-play.

Visit our website at **www.thesavvyactor.com** or call **212-502-0908** to set up your session.

Interviewing well is an art. You should control the interview as much as possible. Show them what you want them to see. The following two pages will help you focus your interview and help you feel more in control.

Stories About Your Credits or Experiences Listed On Your Resume

Have three stories crafted on your resume to reflect the three essences of your brand. If they ask you about a show on your resume that you have not crafted a story around – simply say, "That was a great experience – but when I did this other show…." Lead them to what you want them to know.

1.

2.

3.

Three Personal Questions To Ask

When interviewing with someone it is so important to have a dialogue. Have questions prepared to ask the interviewer. Be interested in who they are.

Example: *How did you get into the business?*

1.

2.

3.

Three Business Questions To Ask

Here is where you can show your knowledge of who you are and where you fit in this industry. Have three specific business questions ready to go that have to do with your goals.

Example: *I am focused on musical theater right now but I want to branch into TV, what are your relationships like with the networks?*

1.

2.

3.

Closing Statements

It's important to feel out when the interview is coming to a close. Have a question ready to go that will end the interview. This is your time to take control and then gauge how to move forward with this person. Below are three possible questions. Depending on their answer, it will determine how you follow up with that person.

1. How should we proceed?

2. So, what are our next steps?

3. Is there anything else you need from me?

Meeting and Interview Checklist

Preparation is key. You've done your homework. Now, you're ready for your meetings. It's time to put it all together in a package. The following is your checklist for any interview or meeting you attend:

- ❑ **Press Kit (See The Savvy Press Kit Worksheet)**
    - ❑ List of industry contacts who know you and your work
    - ❑ Projects you are right for
        - ❑ Current and upcoming Broadway shows
        - ❑ Off Broadway shows
        - ❑ Regional theater
        - ❑ TV shows
        - ❑ Film: Writers/Directors
    - ❑ "Outside the box" roles
    - ❑ People you get compared to (see your Brand Tally worksheet)
    - ❑ Demo CD or reel (if you have it)
    - ❑ Quotes from reviews

- ❑ **Bring ten copies of your Headshot/Resume** (just in case!)

- ❑ **The 30 Second Blurb,** rehearsed

- ❑ **Interview question responses,** prepared

- ❑ **Three stories** about experiences on your resume

- ❑ **Three business questions** to ask the agent or casting director

- ❑ **Three personal questions** to ask the agent or casting director

- ❑ **Closing statements**

Social networking is a free form of promotion and a way of distributing your brand to the rest of the world.

Actors should look at social networking as social *marketing.* Agents are using it to keep track of their talent, casting directors are using it to cast, and producers are using it when finalizing casting. Believe it or not, it's important to them that you are "Google-able."

What Is Your Social Networking Strategy?

As an actor you should have a presence on at least 3 of the 5 social networking options. Each one of these has a specific use. **Note:** *There are always new sites, so be on the lookout.*

1. **Facebook** (MUST) – Facebook is the number one social networking site and a place to be found and/or reached. Your Facebook page nearly always shows up in your first three Google results, so it becomes a tool for casting directors, agents and producers. We recommend using Facebook as a business tool. Keep in mind there can be a fine line between business and personal. Decide how you'll use it. A Fan Page is an option to keep business and personal use separate.

2. **LinkedIn** (MUST) – This is your business account. You can find out who is in your '6 Degrees' and ask to be introduced. There's more business formality here, which makes it attractive to other professions.

3. **Twitter** (Optional) – People can follow you and, unlike Facebook, you don't have to request or confirm their relationship to you. Using 140 characters you get quick access to people you may not know but want to meet. It's also a great tool to keep in touch with your fans.

4. **MySpace** Music, Comedy, or Filmmaker Pages (Optional) – This is the "space" to get in front of like-minded individuals. Unlike Facebook, MySpace allows you to gear your content to a specific audience. Great for posting MP3's, videos, and upcoming events.

5. **YouTube** (Optional) – Create buzz for yourself by posting your reel, commercials, performance clips, etc. YouTube is great for posting your own content.

6. **Blog** (Optional) If you're a writer, love to write daily or have a great point of view, then you should also start a blog. Wordpress and Blogger are the most popular.

Developing Your Strategy

Because of the nature of social networking, it's important for you to have a system in place. It can get overwhelming and a system will help you decide:

1. How often do you update?

2. What do you update about?

Important: Keep in mind that the goal is to use these social networking sites to direct people to your website.

Use the space below to create your plan. Answer the following questions:

- What am I using this site for (business, personal or both?)
- When and how many times a day/week am I updating it?
- What am I writing about/updating?

1. **Facebook**

2. **LinkedIn**

3. **Twitter**

4. **MySpace**

5. **YouTube**

6. **Blog** (Daily, Weekly)

Savvy **Tip**

Use Social Networking Management Sites/Applications
Social networking management sites help you focus the flow of your various social networking accounts into one place and allows you to update your various social networking accounts all at once, without having to login to each account separately. Check out **Ping.fm.**

Website

Your website is a direct extension of who you are and what you sell. It will also be the first thing that comes up when someone searches for you on the Internet. It has to be consistent with all your other marketing.

Think about it, if you search for a business on the Internet and it's not there – don't you question the caliber of that business? Having a website is becoming a must for actors. Actors need to be searchable. Social networking sites help with that, but you need a site you can officially call your own, where you are in charge of all the content. Your social networking sites are tools to drive traffic to your website. This is where, ultimately, casting directors, agents, and directors can peruse all your best marketing tools, in one place and at a moment's notice.

Creating a Website

A website is where you can have fun and showcase who you are. It must be easy to navigate, without too may bells and whistles. Use the same fonts and color scheme you chose for your resume (Refer back to the soap question on the Personal Brand Breakdown Exercise for ideas). The text on your website should convey the same tone as your cover letters. All of your marketing materials should complement each other. Your essence needs to be consistent.

There are no rules as to how many pages or what they should be, but search around for actors you admire and look at what they are doing on their websites. This will give you some idea of how you want to approach your own. Standard pages include: Homepage, Bio, Resume, Photos, Media (videos, song recordings, reels, etc.), Press and Contact.

If you hire a website developer, make sure they understand the intended experience, the look and feel, of visiting your site. Just like finding a headshot photographer, interview a few people and look at their work before deciding on one.

If you prefer to do it yourself and you're a Mac user, look into iWeb software as an efficient way to build your website.

Savvy Tip

Purchase a brand centric domain.
Hopefully, you have the rights to use "your name.com." If someone already has your domain, you should consider a brand centric domain. Maybe you add a middle initial or craft a domain name that speaks to your brand.

Once you've purchased your new domain, register that domain with Google, Yahoo and Bing to ensure Search Engine Optimization (SEO). This will help to make sure the search engines find your website when a casting director, director, fan, etc. searches for you.

A video reel or audio demo is another strong marketing tool for an actor. They're highly effective representations of you, your brand, and most importantly, your talent. We recommend keeping your reel or demo under two minutes, with your best clips at the beginning.

It's important to show what you do best. Don't use just any clips. And use them strategically. What does a particular clip say about you? What is the story that you want to tell with your clips?

If you're just starting out it's okay to just have a clip or two. The important thing is that you have something. As your career grows, so will the amount of material you have to choose from.

You should have both digital and hard copies. Use digital files for email submissions. Hard copies should be packaged to reflect your overall brand.

Reel

If Film or TV is your goal, then a reel is a smart investment for your career. It allows the industry to see you on screen and get a feel for what you do best. It represents where you fit in the business.

Think of your reel as your personal movie preview. All previews tell a story. What's the story that you want to showcase? How can you tell the story of you in a way that is creative using your existing footage?

Your reel should have your name and contact information on a slate at the beginning and end.

Create a mood consistent with your brand by using appropriate music.

Demo

If musical theater or voiceovers are your thing, a demo is a great tool to represent what you do. Like reels, demos allow the industry to get a feel for what you do best.

Section 5:
Support System

Support System

In order to achieve your goals, you can't do it by yourself. Most of the jobs you'll book will be because of the people you know. You need a team of people around you.

Who do you know?

You never know where you are going to meet people. Of course, there are the obvious places like classes, or through friends of friends. Six degrees of separation between any of us is a reality. If you ask, you shall receive.

These worksheets are about focusing on building a support system for your success as an actor. We've broken your relationships into three distinct categories.

1. **Your Core Team of Advisors** *(See Core Team of Advisors Worksheet)*
   In Savvy Speak, this is your board of directors. These are the people that you can call on for advice, inspiration or mentorship. This includes close family, doctors, teachers, coaches and others whom you can call upon for help.

2. **Your Fans**
   These are the people who root for you and attend your performances; other actors, family, friends, casting directors, directors, etc.

3. **Your Extended Network**
   Friends of friends, these are people still within your circle. This is one area artists often neglect or undervalue. These are people that can make things happen for you like your *uncle's friend in the entertainment industry*. Ask for help and follow up. This is where social networking sites come in handy.

Use the following worksheets to brainstorm the names of any people that fit the respective categories. Think outside of your circle; don't limit yourself to the circle of people you'd normally ask. Don't be afraid to ask anyone for help in meeting someone in the business.

Other possible support system sources

- Alumni networks
- Colleagues/professional contacts

Support System

Write down the names of your fans and who those fans might know.

Fans	Extended Network
Friends, Family, CD's, Directors, etc.	Acquaintances and Friends of Friends

Support System

Write down the names of your fans and who those fans might know.

Fans	Extended Network
Friends, Family, CD's, Directors, etc.	Acquaintances and Friends of Friends

Core Team Of Advisors

	Name	Contact Info
Accompanist		
Accountant		
Acting Coach		
Acupuncturist		
Agent		
Arranger/Transcriber		
Attorney		
Business Card Printer		
Career Coach		
Chiropractor		
Commercial Coach		
Dance Class/Teacher		
Dialect Coach		
Doctor		
E.N.T. Doctor		
Financial Advisor		
Hairdresser		
Headshot Reproduction		
Improv Coach		
Makeup Artist		
Manager		
Massage Therapist		
Nutritionist		
On-Camera Coach		
Personal Trainer		
Photographer		
Shakespeare Coach		
Stylist		
Therapist		
Vocal Coach		
Voice Over Coach		
Voice Teacher		

Enriching Your Support System

Our business is all about building, creating, and maintaining relationships. This can be referred to as networking. Instead of the term networking, we prefer to say *enriching your support system*.

It's easier to enrich your support system when you understand that both parties benefit from your success. You have great gifts to offer. Own that. Confidence is sexy. Desperation is not. Use your support system to alleviate feelings of desperation and to help introduce you to the people you want to meet.

Ways to Enrich Your Support System

- At auditions with other actors.

- In class with your teachers and other actors.

- When you are at show, out to dinner or at a bar — you never know who is sitting next to you.

- At parties.

- Paying to meet people at seminars.

- Networking brunches and events.

- Social networking sites.

- Wherever you can meet and talk to people who are in our industry!

Savvy Resource Center

Use our FREE Resource Center to build and enrich your support system. It has over 40 categories and over 140 entries. Go to **www.thesavvyactor.com** and click on **Resources**.

Brainstorm other specific ways that you can enrich your support system. Where do you meet people? In what situations are you the most social? When are you at your best in connecting with people?

Maintaining Your Support System

We have talked about enriching your support system and building relationships. But it's just as important to maintain those relationships. How are you going to maintain your support system?

Ways to Maintain Your Support System

- Monthly newsletters – let your fans know what you are up to on a monthly basis.
- Email updates – don't want to pay for an HTML newsletter service? Simply send a mass email.
- Facebook events – invite people to your shows, screenings, and TV air dates.
- Blogging
- Think outside the box – schedule a quarterly mixer event and invite your support system out to a bar/restaurant to meet each other.
- Schedule a coffee date twice a month with someone new whose career you admire and find out how they got where they are in their business.
- Create your Savvy Social Networking Strategy (See page under Marketing).
- Create your "movie premiere invitation list" or "theatrical opening invitation list."

What's your strategy to maintain your support system?

We just looked at maintaining your support system. Now, let's specifically look at maintaining a relationship with your agent. Many actors look at the agent relationship as the be-all and end-all, but, really, that's when the work begins, on a different level.

When an actor gets an agent, we often find that one of two things happen:

1. They're at a loss as to how to proceed.
2. They rely too much on the agent, and stop their own self-promotion.

Both of these can hurt the agent relationship.

The Five P's to a Productive Agent Relationship:

1. Proper Setup of Relationship
The first step, mainly with legit representation, is making sure they agree with what you sell. This is why packaging and aligning your brand is so important. If you have done all your branding homework and know where you fit in the industry, and they agree, then the relationship will thrive.

In beginning any business relationship, setting up proper communication is vital. *Do they prefer email, phone, or dropping by? If there is a project you're right for, how should you communicate that?* These are important questions to answer because if you establish the communication style upfront you never have to second-guess or worry when contacting them. When you do contact your agent, it must be for a reason – not just to check in.

2. Peer and Partner Thinking
Your relationship with your agent is a business partnership, it's not a time to be passive! Remember, they only get 10% commission. It is your job to do 90% of the work. It's your career, not theirs.

Think of them as a peer, not an authority figure; ask for what you want and need without fear. Being afraid of your agents is not the way to have a relationship. When you come from a place of fear, you are not being your authentic self. It's harder to function in a productive way.

3. (Be) Proactive
You've got to be proactive with your agents. This means filling them in on what's going on in your career and giving them the tools to sell you.

Tools that "sell" you would be:

- ❏ Feedback you get in the room when you audition.
- ❏ When someone you know is directing/casting/producing/musical directing/writing a project.
- ❏ Casting directors who know you and what they've said about you.
- ❏ Maintaining and updating information on your website and submission sites.

4. Professionalism and `Preciation

You are a small business owner, and it's of the utmost importance to be professional. Actors tend to complain about their agent situations – whether they don't have one or they feel their agent isn't working with them. A small business owner would not complain but rather take steps to fix it. If you treat your agent with professionalism, they will do the same.

Appreciation or gratitude is the key in maintaining relationships and being professional. Thanking your agent for negotiating contracts and getting you in for auditions is just good business practice. Thank you's are a must.

5. Position of Trust

When you start working with an agent in a freelance or signed capacity, both parties are really saying, "I trust you to do your job." The actor must trust that they are being submitted, and the agent must trust that you are doing your best work in the room and being professional.

Yet, agents hear these words countless times -"Can you submit me for this?" What actors don't realize, is by asking this question they are basically saying, "I don't think you did your job, so I have to check up on you." There's a big difference between saying, "Can you submit me for this?" and "I'm sure you submitted me, but I'm very interested in this project" or "I'm sure you submitted me, I just wanted to let you know the director knows my work." By demonstrating trust, your relationship will be based on a foundation of respect and, inevitably, grow.

Section 6:
Finances

We don't believe in the starving artist mentality. But some do. Some actors are more committed to the romantic notion of the struggling artist rather than building a successful business. Some actors are more committed to accepting non-paying acting jobs and relying on credit cards rather than creating a financial plan and budget. We believe that you can be a noble artist and have financial success too.

Finances are the backbone of any business, even an acting career. Having the right financial plan will help you decide when to take class, when you may have to work to survive, or when you can take a vacation. To be successful you need to come to terms with your financial situation, as well as your emotions and your beliefs regarding money.

For many of us our financial education ends after learning how to balance a checkbook. We're not taught how to track our income, expenses or investments. Most people don't really know their bottom line.

> **This section of the manual is included to help you figure out where you are financially. However, *we are not financial advisors*. We are only describing organizational systems for finances that have worked for us.**

Fixed Expenses vs. Variable Expenses

There are two kinds of expenses, fixed expenses and variable expenses. Fixed expenses don't change or fluctuate from month to month. Fixed expenses are your bills: rent, mortgage, utilities, cell phone, cable, student loans, credit cards, web hosting, subscriptions, gym membership, etc. Fixed expenses are paid at regular intervals like monthly, quarterly, or annually.

Variable expenses are expenses that change from week to week or month to month. These include groceries, laundry, eating out, clothes, medical, etc.

Savvy Downloadable Worksheets

Register your Career Manual at **http://www.thesavvyactor.com/RegisterYourManual.php** to receive access to downloadable excel files for the worksheets contained in this section. Some include formulas that will calculate the numbers for you.

1. Fixed Monthly Expenses
2. Fixed Annual Expenses
3. Variable Expenses Tracking Sheet
4. Paycheck Percentage Breakdown
5. Yearly Acting Expense Sheet

Fixed Expenses Worksheet Instructions

Fixed Monthly Expenses Worksheet (page 106)

1. Write down the due date and amount of your monthly fixed expenses – both living and career.
2. Add up the monthly expense column to determine the **Subtotal Of Your Fixed Monthly Expenses.** Write that number at the bottom of the worksheet in the space provided.
3. Take each monthly fixed expense and multiply it by 12 to determine your yearly expense for that particular bill.
4. Add up the yearly amount column to determine the your **Yearly Amount of Fixed Monthly Expenses**. Write that number at the bottom of the worksheet in the space provided.

Fixed Annual Expenses Worksheet (page 107)

1. Write down the due date and amount of your annual, semi annual and quarterly fixed expenses – both living and career.
2. Take each semi annual expense and multiply it by 2 to determine how much you spend yearly for each item. Write that number in the Annual Amount column.
3. Take each quarterly expense and multiply it by 4 to determine how much you spend yearly for each item. Write that number in the Annual Amount column.
4. Add up the entire Annual Amount column to determine the **Subtotal Of Your Fixed Annual Expenses**. Write that number at the bottom of the worksheet in the space provided.

Calculate your Average Weekly Fixed Expenses: (Follow the directions and use the table below.)

1. Add your **Yearly Amount of Fixed Monthly Expenses**, (page 106) to the **Subtotal Of Your Fixed Annual Expenses** (page 107)

Yearly Amount of Fixed Monthly Expenses	
Subtotal Of Your Fixed Annual Expenses +	
Total Yearly Fixed Expenses =	

2. Take your **Total Yearly Fixed Expenses** and divide it by 12 to determine your **Total Monthly Fixed Expenses**. Write that number in the space below.

Total Yearly Fixed Expenses	÷ 12
Total Monthly Fixed Expenses =	

3. Take your **Total Monthly Fixed Expenses** and divide it by 4 to determine your **Average Weekly Fixed Expenses**. Write that number at the bottom of the worksheet in the space provided.

Total Monthly Fixed Expenses	÷ 4
Average Weekly Fixed Expenses =	

This is the weekly amount you need to set aside to take care of your monthly expenses. This is crucial, especially if you're in a cash-based survival job.

Fixed Monthly Expenses

Monthly Fixed Expense Description	Due Date	Monthly Expense	x 12 =	Yearly Amount
			x 12 =	
			x 12 =	
			x 12 =	
			x 12 =	
			x 12 =	
			x 12 =	
			x 12 =	
			x 12 =	
			x 12 =	
			x 12 =	
			x 12 =	
			x 12 =	
			x 12 =	
			x 12 =	
			x 12 =	
			x 12 =	
			x 12 =	
			x 12 =	
			x 12 =	
			x 12 =	
			x 12 =	
			x 12 =	
			x 12 =	
			x 12 =	
			x 12 =	
			x 12 =	
			x 12 =	
			x 12 =	
			x 12 =	
			x 12 =	
			x 12 =	
			x 12 =	

Subtotal Of Your Fixed Monthly Expenses =

Yearly Amount of Fixed Monthly Expenses =

Fixed Annual Expenses - For Living & Career

Annual Fixed Expense Description	Due Date		Annual Amount

Semi Annual Fixed Expense Description	Due Date	Semi Annual Expense	Annual Amount
		x 2 =	
		x 2 =	
		x 2 =	
		x 2 =	
		x 2 =	
		x 2 =	
		x 2 =	
		x 2 =	
		x 2 =	
		x 2 =	
		x 2 =	
		x 2 =	
		x 2 =	
		x 2 =	
		x 2 =	
		x 2 =	
		x 2 =	

Quarterly Fixed Expense Description	Due Date	Quarterly Expense	Annual Amount
		x 4 =	
		x 4 =	
		x 4 =	
		x 4 =	
		x 4 =	
		x 4 =	
		x 4 =	
		x 4 =	
		x 4 =	
		x 4 =	
		x 4 =	
		x 4 =	
		x 4 =	
		x 4 =	

Subtotal Of Your Fixed Annual Expenses =

Variable Expenses Tracking Instructions

Now that you know your fixed expenses, it's time to take a look at your variable expenses. By using the Variable Expenses Tracking worksheet, you'll know what you're spending each week. We recommend tracking your variable expenses for at least three months. You'll be able to average your monthly expenses and track your income to begin to see a clearer financial picture.

This worksheet is not about being frugal, it's about becoming aware of your spending habits. By doing this it will help you plan ahead for the big purchases, a class, a trip, whether you can afford to go away to do summer stock for $300 a week, etc.

The Variable Expenses Tracking worksheet is set up so you will record each day's income, spending and saving habits.

Weekly Forecast Column

The Weekly Forecast column is there to help you forecast your weekly spending habits – how much you anticipate making, saving, and spending. All companies forecast. Like the weather, forecasting is an estimation, based on past experience.

Filling in the Weekly Forecast column:

1. Enter your Average Weekly Fixed Expenses number from page 105
    (Some months have 5 weeks, but don't worry that extra money can be put towards savings)
2. Write down your anticipated income for the week in the Weekly Forecast column
3. Write down your anticipated savings for the week in the Weekly Forecast column
4. Write down your anticipated expenses (the amount you think you will spend) for each category in the Weekly Forecast column.

Again, remember a forecast is a guess at the beginning of each week. It's a test to see how well you know your spending habits.

Daily Columns

Each day enter your expenses, both career and living, and add them up. You will find some days you spend more than others. Ask yourself what was different about those days. Did you eat out? Have class? Etc. We gave you additional space to add categories.

Weekly Total

At the end of the week you will add up your weekly total. You will discover if what you forecasted equaled what you actually spent. It's a huge indicator of your spending habits.

Tracking what you are spending and earning each week allows you to see your monthly picture. Once you have enough information, you can compare previous weeks or months. You will start to see trends in your spending habits and be able to adjust in order to achieve your financial goals. Remember, this is something you'll have to practice. **We recommend doing this daily for at least three months.**

Variable Expenses Tracking

Week of: _____

	Weekly Forecast	Sunday	Monday	Tuesday	Wednesday	Thursday	Friday	Saturday	Weekly Total
Income - Checks/Cash/Tips									
Weekly Fixed Expenses									
Savings									
Breakfast									
Lunch									
Dinner									
Groceries/Home Products									
Snacks/Coffee									
Transportation									
Entertainment									
Clothing									
Laundry/Dry Cleaning									
Toiletries/Makeup									
Gifts/Donations									
Medical									
Misc.									
Acting Publications									
Books/CD's/DVDs									
Business Meals/Gifts									
Business Transportation									
Classes									
Coaching & Lessons									
Equipment: Computer, Phone, etc.									
Events & Seminars									
Advertising/Marketing Materials									
Office Supplies									
Research: Theater/Movies/etc.									
Misc. Acting Expenses									
Totals	Weekly Forecast	Sunday	Monday	Tuesday	Wednesday	Thursday	Friday	Saturday	Weekly Total

Finances

Variable Expenses Tracking

Week of:

	Weekly Forecast	Sunday	Monday	Tuesday	Wednesday	Thursday	Friday	Saturday	Weekly Total
Income - Checks/Cash/Tips									
Weekly Fixed Expenses									
Savings									
Breakfast									
Lunch									
Dinner									
Groceries/Home Products									
Snacks/Coffee									
Transportation									
Entertainment									
Clothing									
Laundry/Dry Cleaning									
Toiletries/Makeup									
Gifts/Donations									
Medical									
Misc.									
Acting Publications									
Books/CD's/DVDs									
Business Meals/Gifts									
Business Transportation									
Classes									
Coaching & Lessons									
Equipment: Computer, Phone, etc.									
Events & Seminars									
Advertising/Marketing Materials									
Office Supplies									
Research: Theater/Movies/etc.									
Misc. Acting Expenses									
Totals	Weekly Forecast	Sunday	Monday	Tuesday	Wednesday	Thursday	Friday	Saturday	Weekly Total

Finances

With all this tracking, you should now have an idea of your actual weekly financial picture. It's time to take that knowledge and create your organizational system. We want to reiterate: *we are not financial advisors*. But we do want to provide you with an organizational system for you to take ownership of your finances.

A lot of people have one savings account and one checking account. Every month they transfer money into their savings account. Towards the end of the month the checking account becomes depleted and anything that was saved gets transferred right back into the checking account. The cycle goes on and on. To break this cycle, we use a system of bank accounts, each with a specific purpose, to organize our money.

Gross Income vs. Net Income

When looking at finances you need to know the difference between gross and net income.

Gross income is your total income before any taxes and deductions are taken out.

Net income is the income remaining once taxes and deductions have been taken out.

Some income is 1099 income. This is gross income paid to a nonemployee or independent contractor. Employers send you a 1099 form instead of a W-2 form at the end of the year. No taxes are taken out of 1099 Income. If you're an independent contractor, it's your responsibility to account for the taxes you owe. We suggest taking 20-30% of that 1099 income and placing it in a savings account to pay any taxes you may owe.

Creating Your Financial System

For the following example we will be dealing with net income.

Account #1 – Retirement Savings – Save 10%

Pay yourself first. Most financial systems start with the premise of paying yourself first. This we'll refer to as your retirement savings. What this means is that for each paycheck you set a certain amount aside for savings. The amount typically recommended to save is 10% of your paycheck. If your check is $1,000, put $100 towards your retirement savings. We recommend having a separate bank account specifically for retirement.

Your retirement savings is something that will continue to grow by letting compound interest work its magic. Use these savings to invest in mutual funds, stocks, bonds and various other investments. As far as investing, it is up to you to do your research. We recommend some excellent books in the Recommended Reading section of our website to get you started.

It's never too early or too late to start thinking about and planning for retirement.

Account #2 – Living Essentials 50% – 75%

You've already started to determine your expenses and income. Now let's figure out the percentage of your income you need to live – your living essentials. By determining the percentage that you need to live, you'll be taking the emotion out of your financial decisions because you will always be covered no matter what. We recommend having a separate account specifically for living essentials. Now, let's calculate the percentage of your income for your Living Essentials Account.

STEP 1: Calculate your Yearly Fixed Expenses Percentage
1. In the space below, write down your **Total Yearly Fixed Expenses** from page 105.
2. Calculate your **Total Annual Income** and write it in the space below. Ideally, you can find this number on last year's tax return. Or, if you've tracked your income for at least four weeks on your Variable Expenses Tracking worksheet, add up your income for those four weeks and multiply the total by 12.

   (If you can, average your last three years of income. It'll help you better account for any inconsistencies that may have occurred. If you're just starting out and have no idea how much you'll make this year start out with an estimated income of $25,000 and adjust from there as you start to better understand your financial picture.)
3. Divide your **Total Yearly Fixed Expenses** by your **Total Annual Income**.

Total Yearly Fixed Expenses	
Total Annual Income ÷	
Yearly Fixed Expenses Percentage =	

Example: $12,000 Fixed Expenses ÷ $35,000 Annual Net Income= .34 or 34%

STEP 2: Calculate your Yearly Variable Expenses Percentage
1. First calculate Your **Total Yearly Variable Expenses**.
   Once you've tracked your expenses for at least one month on your Variable Expenses Tracking worksheet, add up what you spent from the breakfast row to the medical row. ONLY add up the essential living expenses NOT your acting expenses. Once you have this number, your **Average Monthly Variable Expenses,** multiply it by 12 and write it in the space below.
2. Write down your **Total Annual Income** from above in the space below.
3. Divide your **Total Yearly Variable Expenses** by your **Total Annual Income**.

Average Monthly Variable Expenses	X 12
Total Yearly Variable Expenses =	
Total Annual Income	÷
Yearly Variable Expenses Percentage =	

Example: $9,000 Variable Expenses ÷ $35,000 Annual Net Income = .26 or 26%

STEP 3: Calculate Your Living Essentials Account Percentage

Use the table below to determine the percentage you will set aside for living. Transfer the numbers from the previous page. *Example: 34% + 26% = 60%*

Yearly Fixed Expenses Percentage		Yearly Variable Expenses Percentage		Living Essentials Account Percentage
_____	+	_____	=	_____

Your Living Essentials Account Percentage typically will add up to 50 – 75%. (If it's less than 50%, even better.) Again, living essentials include rent, utilities, cell phone, groceries, laundry, etc. This percentage should fulfill your monthly expense requirements. This is why your Variable Expenses Tracking worksheet becomes so important. You may need more or less than 50%. You can always adjust the percentages to suit your financial situation.

Account #3 – Acting Career 15% – 30%

This account is for money that will go towards acting classes, voice lessons, dance classes, headshots, office supplies, etc. Honing your craft never stops. Money needs to be allocated to cover those expenses.

This account can also be for anything that is educational: cooking classes, language classes, financial class, school, etc.

Calculate your Yearly Acting Expenses Percentage

1. Calculate your **Total Yearly Variable Acting Expenses** and write it in the space below. Ideally, you can find this number on last year's tax return. Or, once you've tracked your expenses for at least one month on your Variable Expenses Tracking worksheet, add up what you spent from the acting publications row to the miscellaneous acting expenses row. ONLY add up the acting expenses NOT your essential living expenses.

   Once you have this number, your **Average Monthly Variable Acting Expenses,** multiply it by 12 and write it in the space below.

2. Write down your **Total Annual Income** from the previous page.

3. Divide your **Total Yearly Variable Acting Expenses** by your **Total Annual Income**

Average Monthly Variable Acting Expenses	X 12 =	_____
Total Yearly Variable Acting Expenses	=	_____
Total Annual Income	÷	_____
Yearly Variable Acting Expenses Percentage	=	_____

Example: $7,000 Acting Expenses ÷ $35,000 Annual Net Income = .20 or 20%

Account #4 – Big Purchases

You've finished the calculations. If there's any percentage left over, that's great. It's up to you how to use this income. You can save for a trip, give to charity, have a night on the town, or put towards a new home. We suggest having at least one bank account for this income to save for those big purchases and expenditures.

Remember your total plan must equal 100%. The percentages can be adjusted as needed – you do need to cover your bills. The point is that percentages help make your decisions easier and give you a structure to your finances.

Dedicated Tax Account (Optional) – 20-30% (if they have not already been taken out)

As an actor, you're often paid in 1099 income. Typically this income does not have taxes deducted. As a result, you have to keep track of the tax you owe. We recommend having a separate bank account specifically for taxes.

Create your own Financial System by using the worksheet on page 116.

Use the example on page 115 to see this financial system in action.

Savvy Tip

For great financial book recommendations, check out our Recommended Reading page under resources at **www.thesavvyactor.com**.

Paycheck Percentage Breakdown Example

		Gross Income (1099)	$2,500.00
		Tax 28%	$700.00
		Net	$1,800.00

Account Designation	Institution/ Account Type	% of Check	Account Description	Total
Retirement Savings	ING Savings	10%	Investments Only	$180.00
Living Essentials	Citibank Checking	55%	Rent, Food, Utilities, etc.	$990.00
Acting	Actor's Federal Credit Union Checking Account	20%	Anything Related to Acting	$360.00
Big Purchases	Savings or Money Market	15%	Vacation, New Computer, etc.	$270.00
Tax Account (if necessary)	Citibank Savings	28%	For Taxes if Cash/1099 Income	$700.00

Paycheck Percentage Breakdown

Gross Income	
Tax	
Net	

Account Designation	Institution/ Account Type	% of Check	Account Description	Total
Retirement Savings			Investments Only	
Living Essentials			Rent, Food, Utilities, etc.	
Acting			Anything Related to Acting	
Big Purchases			Vacation, New Computer, etc.	
Tax Account (if necessary)			For Taxes if Cash/1099 Income	

You've tracked your fixed and variable expenses and started to establish your financial system by breaking down your income into percentages. Now, let's get more specific with your yearly acting expenses. The purpose of the Yearly Acting Expenses worksheet is to help you budget for your acting career. As a business owner it's important for you to have a list of all the materials you'll need to have in order to run your business efficiently.

Acting Expenses

1. Multiply your **Total Annual Income** by your **Yearly Variable Acting Expenses Percentage** to find out your acting budget. Both these numbers you already determined in the previous section on page 113.

Annual Income		**Variable Acting Expenses Percentage**		**Yearly Acting Expense Budget**
_____	x	_____	=	_____

Example: $35,000 Annual Net Income x 20% Acting Expense Percentage = $7,000

2. Now that you know how much money you can spend on your acting business, start to budget for your acting expenses. Where will you use the money? What's most important? A new class? Headshots? Going to shows or movies, attending networking events? Focus your money on achieving the goals you have created.

Your finances are the backbone of your business. You need to know how your spending affects your business. Having this financial information will make things easier over the long haul. You'll end up making smarter business decisions.

At the end of the year, add up your actual amount spent and place it in the Actual Column on the Yearly Acting Expenses worksheet located on the next page.

1. Were you right?
2. How much were you over/under?
3. Can you save money anywhere?

This is important information that will help you forecast your future spending.

Yearly Acting Expenses

Acting Yearly Expenses	Budgeted	Actual	Notes
Advertising			
Business Supplies			
Headshots			
Postcards			
Postage			
Business Cards			
Demo Reels			
Website			
Promotional Tickets			
Reference Materials			
Books/Scripts			
Sheet Music			
CD's/DVD's			
Movie Rentals			
Theater Tickets			
Movies			
Concerts			
Museums			
Other:			
Publications			
Backstage			
Variety			
Ross Reports			
Other			
Union Dues			
SAG			
AFTRA			
EQUITY			
OTHER:			
Classes			
Acting			
Voice Lessons			
Seminars			
Coachings			
Accompanist			
Rehearsal Studio			
Computer Expenses			
Hardware			
Software			
iPod			
PDA's			
Video Camera			
Transportation			
Taxis/Transportation			
Other Transportation			
Business			
Business Gifts			
Business Meals			
Other Acting Related Expenses			
Costumes/Makeup			
Total expenses			

When you track your yearly acting expenses, you can also use the information to itemize your deductions on your tax return.

Receipt Filing System

Having a filing system for your receipts makes itemizing your deductions even easier.

- Get a 13-tab expandable file folder and use the categories on the following worksheet (page 120) for each tab. File your receipts daily or once a week, whatever works for you. But file them!

- Before you do, it's important to write on the back of the Starbucks receipt – "Had coffee with Kevin and discussed my monologue." Or on the taxi receipt – "Full Monty audition." If you get audited, you'll have a written record of the receipt's validity.

Unsure of what you're entitled to deduct? Use the Yearly Acting Expenses worksheet as your guide to what may be deductible. Then *make sure* you contact an accountant *who specializes in preparing actor tax returns*.

Volunteer Income Tax Assistance (VITA)

VITA is an IRS-sponsored tax assistance program. It is run on a volunteer basis by IRS-trained members and provides free tax preparation. Members of Equity and other performing arts unions are eligible for this service. Scheduling starts in February, and appointments are by lottery.

Disclaimer: Any financial information discussed in this section is purely for organizational purposes. Be sure to check with your financial advisor/accountant before claiming deductions and filing your taxes.

Savvy **Tip**

Use **Quicken** to keep track of your finances. It's a great tool to organize and calculate your expenses for tax time. For a free option, check out Mint.com.

Business Receipts Filing Portfolio

We recommend purchasing a 13-tab expandable file folder and using the following categories to help you file your receipts:

1. **Advertising/Marketing Materials**- headshots, resume paper, postage, postcards, business cards, website, etc.

2. **Office Supplies** - resume paper, printer ink, pens, staples, binders, sheet protectors, etc.

3. **Classes, Lessons, Events and Seminars**

4. **Scripts, Scores, Books, CD's, DVD's**

5. **Costumes and Make-Up** - tricky category but you are allowed some deductions.

6. **Union Dues and Agent Commissions**

7. **Professional Research** - movie tickets, theater tickets, cable TV, Backstage, Variety, etc.

8. **Business Gifts, Meals, and Meetings,** - coffee with your friends at Starbucks where you discussed how fabulous your audition was, holiday gifts for your agent, etc.

9. **Transportation** –public transportation, gas, cab rides to and from auditions, etc.

10. **Equipment** - computer, cell phone, pitch pipe, software, etc.

11. **Phone** - cell phone calls

12. **Out of Town –** business travel for auditions and work

13. **Donations**

Section 7:

Organizational Systems

Using systems takes the emotion out of your business decisions and allows your creative self and your art to thrive.

In this career manual you have already created systems for goals, branding, marketing, and finances. The key component that supports all of this is your Organizational System.

Actors spend a lot of their days out of the office, if you will, at auditions, coachings, classes, day jobs, rehearsals, etc. To stay organized, you need a system. And it needs to be mobile.

The Savvy Organizational System Components

You have already organized your calendar and tasks, but it is time to take it a step further. The next few pages will help you get a handle on everything, including:

- The Savvy Weekly Checklist
- The Savvy Portfolio
- Mobile Office
- Home Office
- Computer Filing
- Email Organization
- Audition Tracking
- Audition Quantification

Savvy Downloadable Worksheets

Register your Career Manual at **http://www.thesavvyactor.com/RegisterYourManual.php** to receive access to downloadable excel files for the worksheets contained in this section.

1. Savvy Weekly Checklist

2. Savvy TV/Film Audition Quantification

3. Savvy Commercial Audition Quantification

4. Savvy Theater Audition Quantification

The Savvy Weekly Checklist

You've determined your goals, projects, and tasks. Your calendar is up and running. Your task list is categorized and efficient. There is one more system to make your business run smoothly – the Savvy Weekly Checklist.

Some of your tasks will be recurring; they may happen more than once a week. *For example* - working out, vocalizing, writing in your journal, etc. The Savvy Weekly Checklist is an excellent tool to see all your weekly recurring tasks, how often you want to do them, and for how long. This includes craft, rehearsing, working out; anything that has to do with honing your craft, building your business, and keeping you in shape physically, mentally, and spiritually.

An actor's schedule can be sporadic. It can be a challenge to schedule things in your calendar on a consistent basis. A checklist serves as a daily reminder of what you commit to accomplish each week toward your goals. You must make sure you're taking the time to schedule these things in your week.

The Savvy Weekly Checklist Instructions
Use our example on the following page as a guideline.

1. Start by looking at your project and task list and find all the recurring tasks.

2. Brainstorm the other activities you want to do to keep your craft, business, body, and mind in shape. Include down time.

3. Write these events under the appropriate column in the spaces provided. *If an activity occurs three times a week, then write it down three times.*

4. Write how many hours a week you are committing to this activity.

5. Once your week has begun, or things become a bit more concrete, you can then schedule the activities on your checklist by moving them into your calendar. This ensures that you will set aside the time to accomplish them.

6. Once you complete an activity check it off.

7. At the end of the week add up how many hours you worked on your business.

Savvy Tip

In order for your system to function you must keep it organized and up to date.

Take at least one hour on a Saturday or Sunday to comb through your task list and move those tasks that are now time appropriate into your calendar for the coming week. Look at your weekly checklist as well and schedule those events.

The Savvy Weekly Checklist Example

Rehearsal	hrs	Enriching Your Support System	hrs	Read/Writing/Organizing	hrs	Health/Body/Spirit	hrs
☐ Vocalize	0.5	☐ Industry Networking Seminar	2	☐ Success Journal	.25	☐ Yoga	1.5
☐ Vocalize	0.5	☐ Coffee with Friend	1	☐ Success Journal	.25	☐ Yoga	1.5
☐ Vocalize	0.5	☐ Coffee with Friend	1	☐ Success Journal	.25	☐ Cardio	1
☐ Vocalize	0.5	☐ See A Show	3	☐ Success Journal	.25	☐ Cardio	1
☐ Vocalize	0.5	☐ See A Friend's Show	3	☐ Success Journal	.25	☐ Weights	1
☐ Practice Songs	0.5	☐ Talk to Mom and Dad	.5	☐ Success Journal	.25	☐ Weights	1
☐ Practice Songs	0.5	☐ Go to an Open Mic Night	1.5	☐ Success Journal	.25	☐ Meditate	.5
☐ Practice Songs	0.5	☐ MasterMind Group Meeting	3	☐ Read Rich Dad, Poor Dad	1	☐ Meditate	.5
☐ Work on Monologues	0.5	☐		☐ Read Rich Dad, Poor Dad	1	☐ Meditate	.5
☐ Work on Monologues	0.5	☐		☐ Read Rich Dad, Poor Dad	1	☐ Acupuncture	1
☐ Cold Reading Skills	0.5	☐		☐ Organize Upcoming Week.	1	☐ Date Night	4
☐ Cold Reading Skills	0.5	☐		☐ Taking Care of Emails	.5	☐ Stretch	.5
☐ Dance Class	1.5	☐		☐ Taking Care of Emails	.5	☐ Stretch	.5
☐ Dance Class	1.5	☐		☐ Taking Care of Emails	.5	☐ Stretch	.5
☐ Vocal Coaching	1	☐		☐ Taking Care of Emails	.5	☐ Stretch	.5
☐ Career Coaching	1	☐		☐ Taking Care of Emails	.5	☐ Stretch	.5
☐		☐		☐		☐ Take Dog to Dog Park	.25
☐		☐		☐		☐ Take Dog to Dog Park	.25
☐		☐		☐		☐ Take Dog to Dog Park	.25
Total hours	**11** hrs	**Total hours**	**15** hrs	**Total hours**	**8.25** hrs	**Total hours**	**16.75** hrs

123

©2010 The Savvy Actor®

Organizational Systems

The Savvy Weekly Checklist

Rehearsal		Enriching Your Support System		Read/Writing/Organizing		Health/Body/Spirit	
☐	hrs	☐	hrs	☐	hrs	☐	hrs
☐	hrs	☐	hrs	☐	hrs	☐	hrs
☐	hrs	☐	hrs	☐	hrs	☐	hrs
☐	hrs	☐	hrs	☐	hrs	☐	hrs
☐	hrs	☐	hrs	☐	hrs	☐	hrs
☐	hrs	☐	hrs	☐	hrs	☐	hrs
☐	hrs	☐	hrs	☐	hrs	☐	hrs
☐	hrs	☐	hrs	☐	hrs	☐	hrs
☐	hrs	☐	hrs	☐	hrs	☐	hrs
☐	hrs	☐	hrs	☐	hrs	☐	hrs
☐	hrs	☐	hrs	☐	hrs	☐	hrs
☐	hrs	☐	hrs	☐	hrs	☐	hrs
☐	hrs	☐	hrs	☐	hrs	☐	hrs
☐	hrs	☐	hrs	☐	hrs	☐	hrs
☐	hrs	☐	hrs	☐	hrs	☐	hrs
☐	hrs	☐	hrs	☐	hrs	☐	hrs
☐	hrs	☐	hrs	☐	hrs	☐	hrs
☐	hrs	☐	hrs	☐	hrs	☐	hrs
Total hours	hrs	**Total hours**	hrs	**Total hours**	hrs	**Total hours**	hrs

Organizational Systems

It is so important to have your materials with you at all times. You never know when you are going to need a headshot, a business card, a casting director's address, etc. The Savvy Portfolio organizes all of this.

The Savvy Portfolio

The Savvy Portfolio is the main component of your mobile office. To create your Savvy Portfolio, you need at least a 7-pocket expandable file folder with the following categories labeled:

- ❑ Headshots

- ❑ Audition Notices/Checklist – carry hard copies of your audition breakdowns for the next two weeks as well as your Savvy Audition Checklist (see page 135).

- ❑ Sides/Copy/Songs/Monologues

- ❑ Goals – keep your goals, projects and organized task list on you for reference.

- ❑ Follow up – includes your postcards, thank you cards, business cards, stamps, and 9x12 envelopes for headshots.

- ❑ Acting Business – contains your list of support team, press kit, networking events, ideas you have, shows you want to see, plays or books you want to read, etc.

- ❑ Industry – holds the contact information for industry, rehearsal spaces, and audition centers.

Be creative with your portfolio.

Make it your own, so you'll never want to leave home without it.

Savvy Tip

Make office hours for yourself.

Once you set them up, you'll need to maintain these systems. Create office hours for yourself, to stay on top of your business and keep it running smoothly.

Here are two options for creating a mobile office, low tech or high tech. The high tech version is the most optimal, but either way you'll feel savvy with your own office on the go. The important thing is to be organized and portable. Regardless of your system, your mobile office includes your Savvy Portfolio.

Low Tech Mobile Office

- ❑ Savvy Portfolio

- ❑ A notebook to keep track of all your auditions: whom you auditioned for, what you wore, what material you used, what headshot you used, etc. (See Audition Tracking page 129)

- ❑ A flash drive with your resume, bio, headshots, music repertoire, monologues, database of industry contacts, etc.

- ❑ Calendar/planner

- ❑ Business cards

- ❑ Cell phone

- ❑ Pens, highlighters and a stapler.

High Tech Mobile Office

- ❑ Savvy Portfolio

- ❑ A smart phone (Palm, Blackberry, iPhone, etc.) with the ability to check email.

- ❑ Laptop computer with all your goals, acting business, professional research, calendar, resume, bio, headshot, industry database, etc.

- ❑ A Send Out Cards account to do your follow up postcards and thank you cards online.

- ❑ iPerform with The Savvy Actor Industry Database.

- ❑ A flash drive with your resume, bio, headshots, music repertoire, monologues, database of industry contacts, etc.

- ❑ Business cards

- ❑ Pens, highlighters and a stapler.

- ❑ Desk area with comfortable chair

- ❑ Computer with Word, Excel, PDF reader, and a photo editing program

- ❑ External hard drive to back up your computer

- ❑ Printer, scanner, fax, copier (all-in-one or separately)

- ❑ Label maker

- ❑ Three ring binders to organize music, monologues, copy, etc.

- ❑ Filing cabinet for all your contracts, union info, resources, banking, bills, income, financial records, sides, songs, scenes, etc.

- ❑ Envelopes for headshots, pre-stamped with return address.

- ❑ Stack of headshots and resumes ready to go.

- ❑ Other supplies: resume paper, postage, postcards, business cards, paper clips, printer ink, pens, highlighters, staples, stapler, binders, sheet protectors, paper cutter, 3-hole punch, etc.

- ❑ Your calendar and contacts backed up on your home computer if you have a PDA.

- ❑ Make Broadwaystars.com or Variety.com your home page to stay up to date on industry info.

- ❑ Use online banking or Quicken so you can see your accounts whenever you need.

- ❑ A 13-tab expandable file folder for organizing your receipts for taxes. Keep receipts for everything.

- ❑ HD Camera

Savvy Coaching

Need help organizing your business office?

Call us at **212-502-0908** and we will have one of our career coaches walk you through setting up your organizational systems. Just let us know if you're Mac or PC based.

Computer Filing System

Create folders on your computer to stay organized. We recommend the following folders, but you can adapt this to suit your individual needs.

- Acting Business
- Goals
- Mailings
- Industry Databases
- Website Content
- Monologues, Sides, & Songs
- Finances
- Marketing Materials
    — Cover letters
    — Resumes
    — Bios
    — Headshots
    — Press Kit

Email Organization

An inbox with hundreds of emails is overwhelming. We recommend organizing emails into folders for maximum efficiency. Your emails will be easier to search, especially those you need at a later date. We suggest starting with the following folders. Adapt this system and create your own folders to suit your needs.

1. Articles – Emails with articles or links that you'd like to read or follow up on later.

2. Events – Emails with links to events that you want to attend.

3. Acting – Emails that contain information important to your acting career (receipts, classes, auditions, bookings, etc.).

4. Reference – Emails you may need to refer to at a later date (financial, logins, receipts, etc.).

5. Save For Later – Emails that need action… just not today.

6. On Hold – Emails that are waiting for a response.

Audition tracking is really tracking your effectiveness, how well you're doing in the business. It's a key component of your research. By examining *all* aspects of your brand and marketing strategy, you'll see clear trends in your success. You'll be able to identify what is working and what isn't.

Tracking The Actual Audition

The following are the vital statistics that you should track for each audition you go on.

- ❑ What you sang and/or monologue you used
- ❑ What headshot you used
- ❑ What you wore
- ❑ How you wore your hair and makeup
- ❑ Who was in the room
- ❑ Who was the accompanist
- ❑ The address of the casting personnel
- ❑ Feedback or comments from the people in the room
- ❑ Your personal feedback
- ❑ Where the audition occurred

Audition Tracking Tools

- ❑ A notebook
- ❑ An Excel spreadsheet
- ❑ Audition tracking books
- ❑ Online tools and apps

Savvy Tip

Here are some reputable self-submission sites. Most offer listings for both LA and NY.

1. **ActorsAccess.com** – Pay for a Showfax yearly subscription and your Actors Access submissions are free.
2. **Nowcasting.com** – TV (occasionally) and student films/extra work
3. **Mandy.com** – Film work
4. **CastingNetworks.com** (LACasting.com & NYCasting.com) – mostly Student/indie Non-union film and commercial work
5. **Backstage.com** – Theater, musical theater and film
6. **NYCastings.com** – Non-union film and print work

Audition Quantification

Tracking the details of your individual auditions lets you determine how well your headshot and audition material are working. To run your business efficiently, you also need to see a bigger picture and quantify those auditions. When you quantify, you will be measuring the quantity of your submissions vs. auditions vs. callbacks vs. bookings. This information will be invaluable, objective feedback, imperative to refining your business plan. It will be the difference between knowing what works and what feels like it's working.

Quantification Worksheets

There are three worksheets to use, depending on your specific goals.

- Savvy TV/Film Audition Quantification

- Savvy Theater/Musical Theater Audition Quantification

- Savvy Commercial Audition Quantification

Answer the following questions to quantify your auditions and self-submissions by plugging in the numbers on the following worksheets.

a. How may times did you self-submit for an audition? Write the total in the space provided. Make sure to break down the number for each audition site to determine how well each site is working for you.
b. How many auditions did you go on in month? Write the total in the space provided. Break down the source of each audition: agent submission, self-submission, open call, etc.
c. How many callbacks came out of those auditions? Write the total in the space provided. Break down the source of each callback: agent submission, self-submission, open call, etc.
d. How many callbacks resulted in a booking? Write the total in the space provided. Break down the source of each booking: agent submission, self-submission, open call, etc.

How To Use This Information

The information you'll be recording is key in knowing how to move forward. It will stop you from making changes for the sake of making changes and help you make strategic business decisions.

For Example . . .

If you notice that your submissions on Mandy.com for the last 3-4 months aren't resulting in any auditions, but your headshot works in other areas, then maybe it's time to cancel your subscription.

If you notice your auditions from self-submitting are far exceeding your agent auditions, then it's time to set up a meeting with your agent and check in on that business relationship.

If you notice you get a lot of callbacks, but not a lot of bookings, then it's time to decide if you are going to invest in being coached before each callback and/or to analyze what it is you do differently from the original audition.

The Savvy TV/Film Audition Quantification

	Jan	Feb	Mar	April	May	June	July	Aug	Sept	Oct	Nov	Dec	Total
Total Monthly Self Submissions													
Mail													
Actors Access													
Casting Networks													
NY Castings													
Backstage													
Mandy.com													
Total Monthly Auditions													
Open Calls													
Agent Submissions													
Self Submissions													
Mail													
Actors Access													
Casting Networks													
NY Castings													
Backstage													
Mandy.com													
Total Monthly Callbacks													
Open Calls													
Agent Submissions													
Self Submissions													
Mail													
Actors Access													
Casting Networks													
NY Castings													
Backstage													
Mandy.com													
Total Bookings													
Open Calls													
Agent Submissions													
Self Submissions													
Mail													
Actors Access													
Casting Networks													
NY Castings													
Backstage													
Mandy.com													

The Savvy Theater Audition Quantification

	Jan	Feb	Mar	April	May	June	July	Aug	Sept	Oct	Nov	Dec	Total
Total Monthly Self Submissions													
Mail													
Actors Access													
Casting Networks													
NY Castings													
Backstage													
Mandy.com													
Total Monthly Auditions													
Open Calls													
Agent Submissions													
Self Submissions													
Mail													
Actors Access													
Casting Networks													
NY Castings													
Backstage													
Mandy.com													
Total Monthly Callbacks													
Open Calls													
Agent Submissions													
Self Submissions													
Mail													
Actors Access													
Casting Networks													
NY Castings													
Backstage													
Mandy.com													
Total Bookings													
Open Calls													
Agent Submissions													
Self Submissions													
Mail													
Actors Access													
Casting Networks													
NY Castings													
Backstage													
Mandy.com													

The Savvy Commercial Audition Quantification

	Jan	Feb	Mar	April	May	June	July	Aug	Sept	Oct	Nov	Dec	Total
Total Monthly Self Submissions													
Mail													
Actors Access													
Casting Networks													
NY Castings													
Backstage													
Mandy.com													
Total Monthly Auditions													
Open Calls													
Agent Submissions													
Self Submissions													
Mail													
Actors Access													
Casting Networks													
NY Castings													
Backstage													
Mandy.com													
Total Monthly Callbacks													
Open Calls													
Agent Submissions													
Self Submissions													
Mail													
Actors Access													
Casting Networks													
NY Castings													
Backstage													
Mandy.com													
Total Bookings													
Open Calls													
Agent Submissions													
Self Submissions													
Mail													
Actors Access													
Casting Networks													
NY Castings													
Backstage													
Mandy.com													

Section 8:
Resources & Success Strategies

This Resources section is filled with materials that you will be able to draw on to function effectively in your business. Sometimes an acting career can feel like a roller coaster ride – one day you're up, the next you're down. Now that you have your business plan in place, a lot of the unpleasant bumps will disappear, making it a smoother ride. Having success strategies in place will ensure it.

Success Strategies

- The Savvy Audition Checklist
- Success Journal
- Vision Board
- Affirmations

As with the rest of the manual, make this section your own. Use it as a place to put inspiration, goals achieved or anything else that you want to keep as a resource or reference for your business.

Savvy Tip

There will always be plenty to do for your career, but it's important to replenish yourself. Make time everyday to just *be*.

This manual is about crafting your business systems. You're a business owner with a reason and purpose behind everything you do. So why leave things up to fate when you actually get in the door to audition? Auditions deserve a systemized plan as well, so you'll be clear in each and every action you take.

Actors tend to put a lot of pressure on themselves at auditions, which can be self-sabotaging. With the Savvy Audition Checklist (see next page), you'll have your own personalized system to stay focused at auditions and on the path of success.

Audition Checklist Sections:

1. Scheduling the Audition

2. Audition Preparation

3. The Audition

4. Evaluating the Audition

These checklists will serve as your guide when you're most creative or vulnerable. Feel free to use the checklist we've created or design your own. As you systemize every part of your business, do yourself the favor of structuring your audition life. Your instinct and creativity will thrive, knowing you have a system to fall back on.

The Savvy Audition Checklist

Scheduling The Audition

- Is the project something that I want to do? Does it excite me?
- Does the role fit my brand and my type?
- Respond to the call in a timely manner (From Agent, CD, Dir., etc.)
- Get the correct audition details (sides, date, time, place, dress, pay, rehearsal dates, booking dates, etc.)

Audition Preparation

That Week

- Set up coaching(s), vocal, audition, accompanist, rehearsal space, etc.
- Get the sides
- Highlight the sides
- Read the sides
  - Work with someone else
  - Work on camera
- Read sides out loud and get it in my body
- Research the role (movies, recordings, music books, dialect tapes, etc.)
- Time management – to avoid procrastination

The Day/Night before

- Get plenty of sleep (7-8 hours)
- Have outfit ready that fits my brand and role

That Morning/Day

- Warm up (ground myself, stretch, breathe, workout, or sing.)
- Eat a good breakfast
- Positive self-talk and affirmations
- Two headshots, sides, music ready to go in my bag.
- Give myself plenty of time to get to my audition. (Arrive 15 min. early)

The Audition

In the Waiting Room

- Totally focus on audition
- No chatting

In the Audition Room

- BREATHE
- Commit, Commit, Commit
- Be open to adjustments
- Be open to what is being said
- Take my space
- Take control of my audition
- Connect with the reader
- Own the time
- Know I am enough
- Know I am authentic

Evaluate Your Audition

- Positive self-talk & affirmations
- Accept that it's over and let go.
- Record audition in tracking system
- Make accurate self-appraisals
  - What did I do well?
  - What can I change next time?
- Send thank you notes
- What am I grateful for?
- Reward

The Savvy Audition Checklist

Scheduling The Audition

The Audition

In the Waiting Room

In the Audition Room

Audition Preparation

That Week

The Day/Night Before

That Morning/Day

Evaluate Your Audition

Vision Board

You've set your goals, you've created your tasks – now take it a step deeper and make them visual.

A vision board is a collage of your goals and what you want to be, do, and have in your life. It's a poster full of images and words and is as unlimited as your own creativity. It's another tool that works. The more you visualize what you want, the more likely you are to pursue it, and ultimately, to attain it.

A Vision Board Should:

Be visual
Make your vision board as visual as possible, with lots of pictures. Use words and phrases that mean something to you. Images are powerful ways to affect your subconscious mind.

Trigger your passion
Every image on your vision board should elicit a positive emotional response. Your vision board should trigger the passion to achieve your goals every time you look at it. Your vision board is not what you "should" do, but what you want to do.

Be strategically placed
Place your vision board in a location that gives you maximum exposure to be consistently reminded of your desires. Keep it wherever you're sure to see it over and over again; your computer desktop, your song book cover, in your Savvy Portfolio, or even on your refrigerator door.

To create your vision board use images from magazines or the Internet. Sort and cut all the images you find and then arrange/glue them on a poster board. We recommend taking a photo of it so you can use your vision board in more than one place.

Savvy Tip

Update your vision board to keep you inspired. Your vision board should evolve like artwork that shifts and grows with you.

Success Journal

You've done a lot of work in this manual and made important decisions for your business. You are an entrepreneur, blazing your own trail – there is no one like you and no one doing exactly what you are doing. Your journey is unique. Now you have a structure with which to move forward.

Frustrations will arise; your momentum will waver. You'll have days when you wonder what you are doing. Remember the positives in your life. Keep a Success Journal.

What is a Success Journal?

A Success Journal is an excellent tool to keep you moving forward. People tend to gloss over their successes. You have many in a week. Honor them all.

Success Journal Instructions

To begin, get yourself a journal. It can be a beautifully bound blank book, a spiral notebook, a spreadsheet on the computer or a handful of blank pages that you put into this section of your manual.

Everyday write down:

> **Five successes -** A success can be anything that you deem a success. *For example* - I got a callback today, I cooked myself dinner, I walked the dog, I booked a commercial, I did laundry, I worked out, I actually went to the open call, etc.

> **Three things you're grateful for –** There are many studies that show that people who are more grateful have higher levels of well-being and happiness. They feel more in control and are better at coping with stress. Being thankful for what you have and expressing gratitude will keep you moving forward.

The journal really comes into play when you need that extra boost to keep you going. Go back and read it. You'll be amazed at how much you've accomplished, at how many things you have to be grateful for in your life. You will regain your momentum; positive attitudes work.

Affirmations

Affirmations can be powerful tools to align yourself with what you desire. They're phrases said aloud to affirm a belief you want to hold. Using positive affirmations can change the way you think. Trust in them; they work.

How to use Affirmations

Below is a list of affirmations for career, life and finances. If they ring true, use them. If not, write your own. Make sure you state them in a positive, powerful way.

Make saying your affirmations a ritual or a habit. Choose a specific time and place to say them aloud with energy and conviction. If an affirmation feels stale - tweak it or create a new one.

Life

- I attract people in my life that love me and cherish me.
- I am committed to constantly learning and growing.
- I am healthy in all areas of my life.
- I am free to be myself.

Career

- I am calm and confident, free and at ease, passionate and committed in auditions and in life.
- My talent is extraordinary and I am consistently sharing it with the world.
- I trust wholeheartedly in my talent.
- I choose to have a successful acting career. I deserve it and I am worthy of it.
- I have an amazing support system of geniuses.

Financial

- I make money doing what I love.
- I am worthy of being rich and I commit to being rich in wealth and spirit.
- I am excellent at managing my finances.
- I always pay myself first.

Congratulations!

You've completed *The Savvy Actor Career Manual.* Congratulations! You are now a savvy business person.

You hold in your hands your business plan. Refining your business systems is a process. Learn to enjoy the process and give yourself the time to implement your systems and strategies. Your plan will give you the courage to continue moving forward in your journey, even if potential fear of success (or fear of failure) creep in.

Just remember:

1. Your plan will change, it's inevitable. As your dreams manifest, they will do so in unexpected ways. Be open to change and the surprises life offers.

2. You will add to your plan as the year goes on. This is a living document, you've given it life. As your business grows, so will your plan.

This is not a go-it-alone business. To be successful you'll need a strong support system around you. It'll take a group of people to bring your plan to fruition.

So recognizing that ourselves, we must thank you, and our other many talented clients, partners, friends and family, our support system. You are our inspiration. We wish you much success.

Your Biggest Fans,

Jodie & Kevin

"Gratitude unlocks the fullness of life. It turns what we have into enough, and more. It turns denial into acceptance, chaos to order, confusion to clarity. It can turn a meal into a feast, a house into a home, a stranger into a friend. Gratitude makes sense of our past, brings peace for today, and creates a vision for tomorrow." **– Melody Beattie**

About the Authors

JODIE BENTLEY is an entrepreneur, career coach, teacher and professional actor in NYC. After graduating with a BFA in Acting from NYU's Tisch School of the Arts at the Stella Adler Conservatory, she discovered her other loves – sales and marketing. Jodie built her own highly successful sales and marketing company from the ground up. She cultivated years of experience in targeted branding, successful sales tactics, and outside-the-box marketing strategies. Her company laid the foundation for her success in the business of acting, and developed her keen eye and savvy gift for helping other actors achieve their own goals. As an actor, Jodie has played leading roles in workshops of new musicals and plays at the York Theatre, New World Stages, The Workshop Theater and all over NYC. Some of her favorite regional roles include: *Annie Get Your Gun* (Annie Oakley), *They're Playing Our Song* (Sonia), *Sylvia* (Sylvia), *Prelude to a Kiss* (Rita). She also works frequently in commercials, soaps, voiceovers and print. www.jodiebentley.com

KEVIN URBAN is a professional actor and career coach whose entrepreneurial passion is to empower clients to achieve their dreams. A graduate of Elizabethtown College with a BA in Communications focusing on PR, marketing, and theater, he complemented his studies by performing and swimming competitively. These disciplines taught him to set goals and achieve them through practice, patience and persistence; ultimately laying the groundwork for his coaching. Upon graduation, Kevin honed his financial and business skills while working in marketing and business development for Sikorsky Credit Union. As a teacher and coach, he is committed to bringing new and innovative ideas in marketing and branding to the acting community, focusing on graphic design, social networking, and any new technology that makes life easier (particularly all things Apple.) As an actor, Kevin has performed since the age of five, working in theater, TV, film, and commercials. www.kevinurban.com

CPSIA information can be obtained
at www.ICGtesting.com
Printed in the USA
LVIW020857030213

318390LV00009B